Making a **difference** 3

Making a difference 3

Individual Cognitive Stimulation Therapy
A manual for carers
(Making a Difference Volume Three)

First published in 2015

Hawker Publications Culvert House, Culvert Road, London SW11 5DH
Tel: 020 7720 2108 Fax: 020 7498 3023
Website: www.careinfo.org

Printed and bound in Great Britain by Berforts Information Press

British Library Cataloguing in Publication Data
A catalogue record for this book is available from the British Library
ISBN 978 1 874790 69 3

Typesetting by Prepare to Publish Ltd
mail@preparetopublish.com

Also published by Hawker Publications:

Making a Difference
Aimee Spector, Lene Thorgrimsen, Bob Woods, Martin Orrell
2006 ISBN 978 1 874790 78 5
For contact details see above

Making a Difference 2
Elisa Aguirre, Aimée Spector, Amy Streater, Juanita Hoe, Bob Woods and Martin Orrell
2012 ISBN 978 1 874790 98 3

Contents

iCST sessions

Contents

Welcome

Over many years of working in the field of dementia care, I have met many carers who would like to **make a difference.** They want to improve the quality of life of the person they are caring for. They would like to reduce the long periods of inactivity that, sadly, are too common, and provide opportunities for engaging in meaningful and stimulating activities.

It's not easy, of course, to have a lot of time free to engage in these activities but interestingly recent studies show that engaging in cognitive stimulation activities can help make a real, lasting difference in the quality of life of people with dementia. I have no doubt that carers who become involved in offering the programme described in this manual will take a small, but important step to achieving this goal.

It's simple and straightforward

There is no special equipment that's required; carers don't need to have special qualifications or attend long training courses. All that's needed is to spend time with the person with dementia, in a quiet room, for 30 minutes, three times a week for 25 weeks. Although one person may take the leading role in working with the person with dementia, other people in the person's life, such as grandchildren or regular visitors, can also be involved. All however must be prepared to follow the key principles of the approach (described on page 6), which we know are essential for the programme to be useful.

It's effective

The programme, as described here, has developed and evolved from the findings of a number of research studies carried out internationally over the years. People taking part in cognitive stimulation report increased quality of life relative to those receiving usual care, and they typically improve on tests of memory and other abilities. The effects appear to be in addition to those of any medication the person is receiving for dementia. Carers can be confident that this programme is based on the best evidence on what makes a difference for people with dementia.

It's enjoyable

Just as important, these activities can be great fun and enjoyable! It's great to be able to relax and laugh alongside the person you are caring for, to see the funny side of a situation together, to see beyond the dementia and enjoy real quality time together. It can be hard work sometimes, of course; but the experience so far has been that it's a very rewarding programme to be involved in. I hope that's your experience too!

Bob Woods Professor of Clinical Psychology of Older People Bangor University

Key principles of iCST

This manual has been developed in order to provide you with a brief guide for each session, acknowledging that carers and families of people with dementia are experts in their role. The aim is to highlight practical skills and support you in providing opportunities for your relative/friend to be involved in meaningful activities, keeping their mind active and engaged. iCST is based on 13 Key Principles, described in the box. While it is important to follow the activities for each session, it is *essential* that these key principles are followed in the delivery of the sessions. We hope that these will enable you and your relative/friend to enjoy and make the most of the programme.

Key principles of iCST

- 1 Mental stimulation
- 2 Developing new ideas, thoughts and associations
- 3 Using orientation in a sensitive manner
- 4 Focusing on opinions, rather than facts
- 5 Using reminiscence as an aid to the here and now
- 6 Providing triggers to support memory
- 7 Stimulate language and communication
- 8 Stimulate every day planning ability
- 9 Using a 'person-centred' approach
- 10 Offering a choice of activities
- 11 Enjoyment and Fun
- 12 Maximising potential
- 13 Strengthening the relationship by spending quality time together

1 Mental Stimulation

The principal aim of iCST is to get people's minds active and engaged. There is strong evidence that following a diagnosis of dementia, people often withdraw from stimulating activities. This leads to further impairment, due to both loss of skills and confidence. You might explain to people that, like any part of the body, the brain needs to keep exercised to remain active. The aim of iCST is to pitch activities so that tasks are not too easy, meaning that people have to make some effort. Equally, pitching things too high can make people feel uncomfortable.

Pitching the level of mental stimulation often involves some trial and error to get it right!

2 Developing new ideas, thoughts and associations

Often with people with dementia, we tend to talk about things from the past. While this can be enjoyable, it often involves recalling information which has been over-rehearsed. This may therefore be less mentally stimulating than thinking about things in new ways and making new meaningful connections.

The aim of iCST is to continually encourage new ideas, thoughts and associations, rather than just recall previously learned information. A good example of this technique is within the ' faces' exercise. Rather than looking at one face and asking the person what they remember or think about the face, show more than one face and ask questions such as "What do they have in common?", "How are they different?", "Who would you rather be?". Similarly, rather than introducing discussion topics likely to have been covered before, such as "What do you think of the Royal Family?", encourage discussions about new topics such as "Is modern art really art?" or "What do you think of same sex weddings?". These techniques enable people to apply their knowledge, yet develop thoughts and ideas that they may not have had previously, increasing the level of stimulation within the activity.

3 Using orientation in a sensitive manner

Orientation is an important goal of iCST, but the way that people are orientated is key. Rehearsal of orientation information (such as the date) and putting the person on the spot with direct questions (e.g. what is the address?) can be demoralising. Orientation needs to be done in a subtle way at the beginning of each session, for example through conversation about forthcoming festivals, important dates or the weather. Orientation can also be introduced into the topic (such as using summer fruits in a 'food' session).

4 Focusing on opinions rather than facts

An important aim of iCST is focusing on the person's strengths. If we focus on 'facts' too much, there is the risk that people will often be wrong. If we ask people for their opinions, then they may be amusing, sad, unusual, controversial or puzzling, but they cannot be wrong. Everyone is entitled to their own opinion, of course. So, rather than say "Where did you go on holiday when you were a child?" (a memory question), ask "What is your favourite place to go on holiday?" or "Where would you advise a young family to go on holiday?". Rather than ask "Who is the Prime Minister?", ask "What do you think of politicians?" or "Who has been the best leader of the country?", by giving a range of names, backed up by photographs. The activities should never feel like a memory test, and we should avoid asking direct questions of memory such as "Can you remember...?". Reducing the demands of an activity creates an environment that promotes involvement and success.

Key principles of iCST

5 Using reminiscence as an aid to the here and now

Using past memories is very useful during the sessions and can be an enjoyable activity. We can use reminiscence to celebrate the person's family life, personality, career, hobbies and achievements. We need to remember though that sometimes people may have unhappy (even traumatic) memories of their earlier life, and some sensitivity is needed not to push our relative/friend into exposing painful memories. The better we know the backgrounds and life stories of the person, the less likely this is to occur. However, reminiscence can also be a useful tool towards orientation, which is a key goal of iCST. Many iCST sessions allow you to compare old and new, thinking about how things have changed over time. For example, old and new coins and the changes in value of goods can be discussed in 'money' sessions.

6 Providing triggers to support memory

Multi-sensory cues are really important, as memory works much better if you do not rely on just one sense. Try to have a mix of activities involving vision, touch, hearing, taste and smell. Often it is a combination of senses that is most effective. For example, the 'food' session is enhanced if the person can taste, smell and feel food with interesting textures. Words in a discussion may soon be lost when memory is limited. Having an object, a photograph or picture keeps the person's attention on the activity and encourages a focus. Using stimuli, objects, and the paper-based activities provided in this programme will allow us to create an environment that promotes success.

7 Stimulate language and communication

There is evidence that language skills improve when engaging in mentally stimulating activities. Many of the sessions stimulate language, for example naming people and objects (e.g. in categorisation), thinking about word construction and word association. An important goal of iCST is to enhance communication, and make time to listen. It is important to consider if your relative/friend has any hearing or vision problems or if English is not their first language. Sitting next to them whilst engaging in the activities, and making sure they have their glasses and hearing aid is very important.

Key principles of iCST

8 Stimulate everyday planning ability

Skills in planning, organising and sequencing – also known as 'executive functioning' skills, are often very impaired in dementia. Several sessions exercise these skills, for example planning and carrying out stages of a task (making a cake in 'being creative', selecting food for a meal in 'food'). Mental organisation skills are exercised through the discussion of similarities and differences, and through organising items into categories. These subtle tasks should encourage people to use skills which may have become under-used.

9 Using a 'person-centred' approach

In a person-centred approach, we see the person first and foremost, the unique qualities of the individual as determined by their life history. The experiences that have shaped their personality and attitudes lead to a variety of skills, interests, preferences and abilities. The main purpose of iCST is to increase the person's pleasant experiences, by focusing on their strengths, and not concentrating on areas of difficulty. We show respect to the person by getting to know what is important for them, value the diversity of their views, opinions and beliefs, and therefore allowing the person to be different.

10 Offering a choice of activities

This programme is fairly detailed, primarily to make it more user-friendly. It is important that you offer your relative / friend several choices and alternative activities if those described in this manual do not suit their preferences, likes or dislikes. Offering choice allows people to become involved in making the programme their own. We propose that you work together to identify activities that suit the person's interests. For each session, we have suggested a choice of activities (described as **Level A** and **Level B**). Usually **Level B** activities are more demanding on the person's memory and other cognitive skills. Choose the level that is most appropriate and enjoyable for your relative/ friend, or mix activities from the two levels and add your own ideas! Note down activities you have tried for each session, so that next time around they can be among the choices open to you.

11 Enjoyment and fun

If you find people commenting that "this is like being back in school", something is going wrong! This may imply that they are being made to work hard in a strict and serious atmosphere. The activities should provide a learning atmosphere which is fun and enjoyable. Yes, people's brains should be stimulated, but so should their laughter muscles! If the person makes comments about 'school', ask them what they liked and disliked about school, and reflect on whether you are taking on the role of 'teacher' too readily. A key principle of the programme is that activities should lead to your relative / friend feeling enabled and empowered.

12 Maximising potential

There is evidence that people with dementia can learn, with the right encouragement and support. We should be careful therefore not to assume a person is unable to contribute or carry out an activity because they were not able to yesterday or last week. People with dementia often function below their full potential, due to a lack of stimulation or opportunity. An important goal of iCST is that it works by building on the memory and cognitive skills of the person, providing them with the opportunity to practice these skills. This involves giving the person time, being careful not to overload or overwhelm them with information, and providing just enough prompting to enable them to carry out the activity themselves. This will increase exposure to success, which will aid learning and enjoyment. People are more likely to achieve their potential by doing rather than sitting passively and watching.

13 Strengthening the relationship by spending quality time together

The sessions will help strengthen relationships – especially if we do not become 'teachers', but assist the person, to join in, and have fun. An important aspect of iCST is that it gives other family members or friends an opportunity to feel at ease, and enjoy quality time together. The true focus is not about the activity itself, but the quality and joy of the interaction. You are also encouraged to set time aside to celebrate your role as a carer. Providing a caring, happy and fulfilling environment for your relative/friend is a rewarding experience and we hope this programme helps carers to achieve this.

How to use this manual

This manual is a step by step guide to delivering Individual Cognitive Stimulation Therapy, or 'iCST'. You will find detailed guidance for each activity, including the structure of the session and ideas for activities and discussion topics.

How many sessions are there, and how long do they last?
In this manual there are 75 iCST activity sessions in total. We suggest that you and the person complete **three iCST sessions per week**. Each session should last approximately **20-30 minutes**.

How are the sessions structured?
The structure for each session is always the same, which includes an opening discussion of the weather and current events (see page 12), followed by the main iCST activity. The activities for each session have been designed to stimulate discussion about different topics. You will also find paper-based resources for many of the activities in this book.

Time and place for iCST
It may be helpful to consider what time of the day is best for you and the person to engage in the sessions together. For example, you might find that it is easier to complete the activities in the morning. You may need to allow some time to familiarize yourself briefly with the activities or prepare materials before each session. Choose a place to do sessions that both you and your friend/relative feel comfortable in. It might be helpful to have access to a table so that you have somewhere to place the resources.

Engaging in activities

Each person has his/her own individual interests, skills, experiences and abilities. Previous research shows that people with dementia can engage successfully in a wide range of meaningful and stimulating activities. A key aim of the iCST programme is to ensure that the person engages in activities that make them feel enjoyment and success. One of the reasons why a person may not enjoy the sessions is that the activities might be either too easy or too difficult for them. It is important to find ways to adapt the sessions if necessary so that there is more for the person to enjoy and feel positive about. We've provided some tips overleaf in the green box.

Getting started

At the beginning of each iCST session we suggest that you and your friend/ relative spend 5-10 minutes 'warming up'. We have provided some ideas for warming up activities and how you can start each iCST session overleaf.

How to use this manual

Brief guide to engagement

- Choose a time of the day to engage in the activities that **'feels right'**
- The sessions should concentrate on **opinions** rather than facts
- **Avoid correcting and emphasising on errors** during the sessions
- **Avoid asking questions that are direct** such as "Do you remember...?"
- Adapt the sessions in order to include your **relative's/friend's interests**
- **Avoid asking questions that involve explicit memory**, such as "Where did you go on holiday last year?"
- Focus on the **person's strengths**
- **Offer an alternative activity** if the first activity does not work

Discuss the day, date, weather, and season

Spend a few minutes discussing the weather. Take a look out of the window together and ask the person what they think of the conditions outside. The idea of this part of the session is to orient the person in a sensitive manner, and guide them through the information. Below are some tips to help you:

- **Use cues:** Use **newspapers, calendars, diaries,** and **clocks** as cues to sensitively orientate the person to information about the season, day, date, and weather.
- **Talk about your plans for the week:** Discuss with your friend/relative activities of the previous week and talk about upcoming events.
- **Useful phrases and questions:** What do you think of the weather today? Is it normal for this time of year? Shall we see if it is anyone's birthday around now?

Discuss recent or current events in the news

Spending a few minutes discussing current events helps to orientate the person to the 'here and now'.

- **Newspaper:** Choose an article from the newspaper and look at it together. Discuss ideas that you have about the news item. You can prepare a brief summary with a news headline and images or a brief summary of the day's current events for your discussion.
- **Local or personal events:** Talk about an interesting or important event that has happened locally, or events related to family and friends.

Start each session with refreshments

Having a drink or a little something to eat together can be a very inviting way to start a session.

Other warming up activities prior to beginning

- Listen to a piece of music or sing along to a favourite song.
- Engage in gentle movement/stretches. Breathing exercises can help with relaxation.

However, do take great care that no one overstretches or strains themselves when engaging in light exercises.

Frequently asked questions

Can we take a break during the session if we need to?
Yes, take time to rest or have refreshments and pick up the session again from where you left off. When you begin again, it might be helpful to review the activities you completed before you stopped. For example, if you were doing a word search together, you could remind your relative/friend of the words you have already found, and discuss the ones you will be looking for next.

What if we don't have time to do a session?
Carers often lead very busy lives and unexpected things may occasionally disrupt plans. If you miss a session due to other commitments, you can just reschedule the session for a more convenient time. You might want to consider involving other family members, such as grandchildren, friends or regular visitors in the programme. When the programme was being developed, carers often mentioned that including other family members in the sessions could be fun, sparked lots of discussion, and made other family members feel good that they were part of the programme.

How do I prepare for the activities and how long will it take?
We recommend that you take some time to have a brief look at what the next session theme is, and the activities provided for that session. This gives you the opportunity to familiarise yourself with the activity or think of alternative ideas if you decide the activities provided will not be enjoyable or suitable to the person's interests.

Should we complete the sessions in the order presented here?
Generally, yes. This manual has been carefully developed with carers and people with dementia, so wherever possible keep to the sessions as laid out. The ideas presented are intended to be suggestions or starting points for discussions. You can use them as a guide, but if you think of your own activities, feel free to be creative! You know the person and their interests best, and what sort of activities will bring them the most enjoyment.

How do I choose which level of activity to do?
Most of the activities are split into 'Level A' and 'Level B'. Level A activities tend to be less challenging than Level B activities. When deciding which level is most appropriate, take

into account your relative's/friend's interests and abilities, and ask them which activity they would prefer to do. You do not have to follow a particular level throughout the whole programme. Each individual has different abilities, so may work at Level A in one skill area, such as communication, but Level B in another, such as numeric skills.

How long should we spend on each activity?
There is no specific time limit to any of the activities in the programme, so spend as much or as little time as necessary on each. You should judge when it is an appropriate time to 'move on' to the next question or stage in the activity, bearing in mind that it is important to make sure your relative/friend has enough time to think about the questions and discussion points provided. If there are questions that seem too challenging or appear not to engage the person, try another question or move on to a different topic. Each session is designed to last for approximately 20 minutes.

What happens if my relative/ friend gives an incorrect answer?
This is not a problem, as the programme is intended to focus on opinions rather than facts. The activities are designed so that there is often more than one answer and less emphasis on right or wrong. It is often our instinct to correct mistakes, but it is important to resist this to prevent your relative/friend feeling under pressure or demoralised. For example, if the person says they think a landscape is in Italy, but you know it is in France, there is no need to say that they are 'right' or 'wrong'. Rather you might say "So you feel that this picture shows a place in Italy". You might then discuss what it is about the picture that makes the person think of Italy when they see it.

What if my relative/friend is not interested in the session theme?
Everyone has different interests so it is natural that some themes may not be to everyone's taste. If you find this is the case, you may repeat an activity from a theme your relative/friend particularly enjoyed instead. Bear in mind that we don't feel the same every day, so it might be a good idea to try things again on a different day as they might work better at a different time. If your relative/friend becomes distressed or seems unresponsive, it might be his/her own way of responding to something they feel is too challenging for them. If this happens, it might be useful to reflect on what happened in order to plan for the next sessions.

What next?

When you have reached the end of the iCST programme, you can continue, if you wish, by revisiting the sessions you enjoyed most, or create some of your own.

Other types of stimulating activities

There are many other forms of stimulating activities that may also be useful, and will add to the variety of stimulation and experience for the person. These include creative therapies, such as art and painting sessions, music sessions, physical exercise sessions, reminiscence sessions, aromatherapy and hand massage.

Developing new ideas – useful resources

We recommend the following sources of ideas for further activities:

- **Cognitive Stimulation Therapy (CST)**, www.cstdementia.com. The website of CST, providing an introduction to the development, research and provision of Cognitive Stimulation Therapy for people with dementia.
- **Reminiscence: The Robert Opie Collection**, www.robertopiecollection.com. The world's largest collection relating to British Nostalgia and advertising memorabilia
- **BBC On this Day**, http://news.bbc.co.uk/onthisday. News stories from each day across the decades – useful for current affairs and reminiscence
- **Keeping Active and Staying Involved factsheet**, www.alzheimers.org.uk. Alzheimer's Society factsheet on hobbies, pastimes, and everyday activities
- **Activities for Older Adults**, www.elderlyactivities.co.uk A website by The Consortium Care with ideas for home-based activities free to view and download
- **TR Therapeutic Recreation Directory**, www.recreationtherapy.com/tx/actindex.htm. An independent recreation therapy website with useful information and resources on recreational activities

1 | My Life (Life History) I

Level A

Materials needed:

- Old and new family photographs.

Look at old and new photographs of family members or friends and try to generate discussion about them, by arranging them into a timeline or tree.

Things to think about...

- Shared features or traits
- Interesting life stories of family members and friends
- Favourite family members and friends as a child
- Advice about how to maintain good relationships

Level B

Materials needed:

- photos of family members (optional),
- pen, paper.

Create a family tree to record your family's history. Add family members such as brothers and sisters, children, grandchildren, or great grand children etc. to the tree. You can add double lines to show that family members are married. You could also add birthdates, years, or places of birth. You can add as many generations of your family as you like. We have provided an example for you opposite.

Things to think about...

- Birthdates or places of birth to track geographical roots of the family
- Interesting life stories of family members
- How everybody's lives differ with each generation

Example

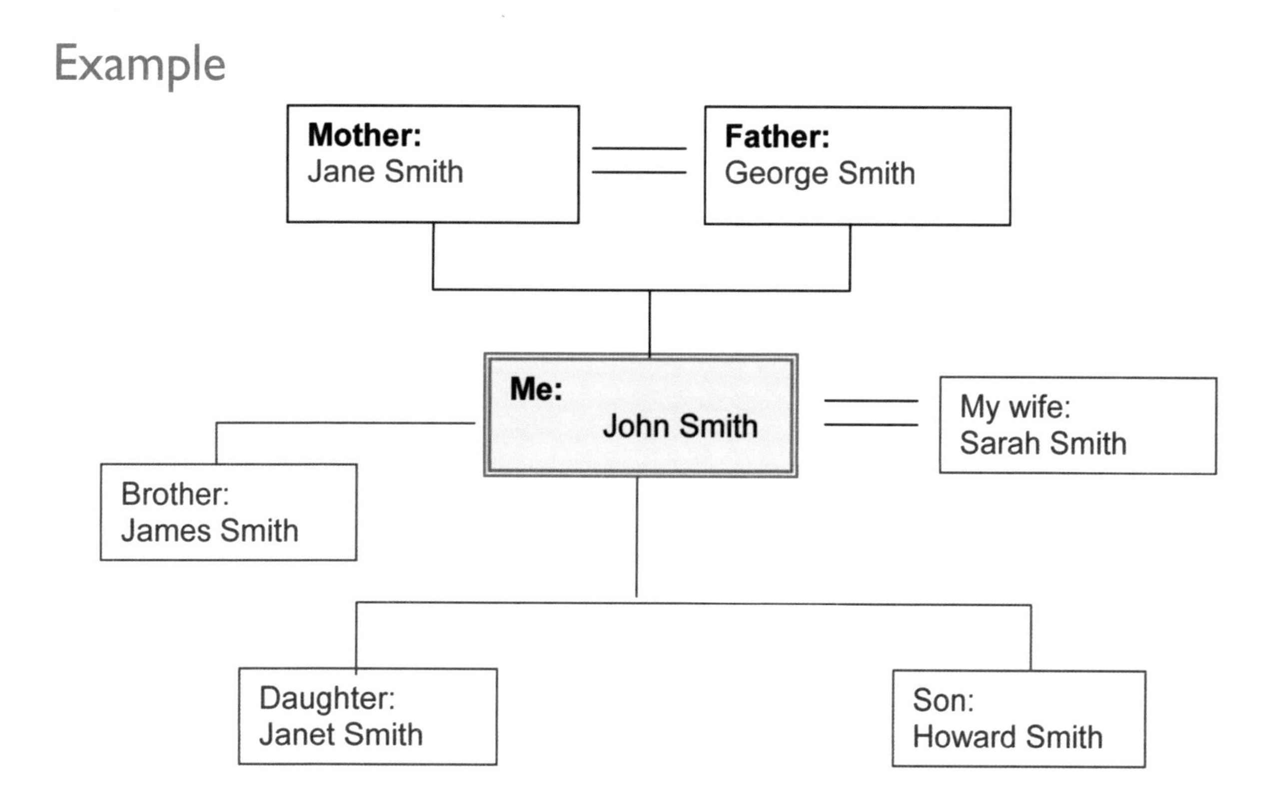
Mother:
Jane Smith
Father:
George Smith
Me:
John Smith
My wife:
Sarah Smith
Brother:
James Smith
Daughter:
Janet Smith
Son:
Howard Smith

2 | My Life (Life History) II

Level A

Materials needed:

- My Life History game board (see opposite)
- a coin or counter (optional).

Place the life discussion game board on a flat surface, such as a dining or coffee table. Take turns to flick or spin a coin on the board. Answer the life question in the box the coin lands on (or nearest to).

If you prefer, just choose a selection of the questions that appeal most to you and the person. You may also add questions of your own. You do not have to answer all of the questions on the board, or any you feel uncomfortable with. It might be nice to share answers – you might find out some interesting facts you never knew about each other!

Level B

Materials needed:

- My Life Now activity sheet (below and opposite).

Use the points on the activity sheet to stimulate conversation about the person's current likes and dislikes. There are no right or wrong answers, and you can add questions of your own. Feel free to write your ideas down, or if you prefer just discuss the topics.

My Life Now activity sheet

What's important to me now

What kinds of things do you like to talk about?

....

....

What do you like to eat and drink?

....

....

What is important to you about your appearance? E.g. clothes, hair, or nails.

....

....

What types of music do you like to listen to?

....

....

What types of radio channels or television programmes interest you?

....

....

Do you have any particular **dislikes** (food/ dress/ activities/conversation topics etc.)?

....

....

My Life History game board

What were you like at school?	Did you enjoy working? What was your favourite job and why?	What makes a good friend?	What would you say your best quality is?
Who is the most influential person you have met or known and why?	What makes you laugh? What makes you happy?	Who have you been closest to in your life? What are their best qualities?	What is your biggest achievement, or your proudest moment?
Does anything scare you?	What was a fun activity to do when you were younger? And now?	What's the best advice you have ever received? FREE ADVICE	What's the most daring thing you have ever done?

My Life Now activity sheet (continued)

How I like to spend my time

Do you like to be part of a group or prefer one to one company? Why?

....

....

What are the things that you particularly enjoy in life? E.g. contact with children or animals, reading a paper, a beautiful garden or going shopping.

....

....

The people who are important to me

Who are the most important people in your life at the moment?

....

....

3 | Current Affairs I

Level A

Materials needed:

- Pen and paper, container (e.g. bowl, bag).

Write questions on slips of paper and put them in a container. Pull out questions at random and discuss the topics. Either use the suggested current affairs topics below, or come up with some of your own.

Suggestions…

- Have the roles of men and women in society changed over the years? Should men do the cooking, cleaning and laundry?
- Is it too easy now to get a divorce?
- Should there be a retirement age for everyone? What should it be?
- What do you think of same sex weddings?
- Is having a Royal Family an asset or an outdated tradition?

Level B

Materials needed:

- Recent newspapers, special supplements, local magazines
- articles sourced from the internet.

Choose a selection of articles about current news stories/current global or local issues that you and the person enjoy discussing.

Things to think about…

- Recent world events
- How events affect people in the area/the wider effect of the event
- Can we learn anything from similar events from the past?

Current Affairs I | 3

4 | Current Affairs II

Level A

Materials needed:
- 50s and 60s newspaper articles (see examples opposite)
- a recent newspaper (optional).

Discuss the news items on the activity sheets, which are based on articles from the 1950s and 1960s. Compare the articles with modern news articles.

Things to think about…
- Do you have any memories of the events featured?
- Views about the war and rationing.
- Views about technology, space travel and science.
- Are there any signs in the articles that society has changed or stayed the same?
- Is the way news is reported different now?
- What types of news items are reported now compared to in other decades?
- What sort of articles do you find interesting and why?

You could source articles from other decades for this activity if you prefer. Your local library may have archived copies of local and national newspapers available to photocopy. You may also be able to find some interesting resources on the internet (i.e. BBC On this Day).

Level B

Materials needed:
- Local newsletters, papers
- letters received in the post (e.g. election candidate information, recycling information), information pamphlets
- images or articles sourced from the internet.

Discuss local news or upcoming events using local literature as a cue.

Things to think about…
- Any local news and how it might impact your community
- Local changes that are likely to take place
- Local policies such as recycling, parking, neighbourhood watch

The Daily News

No. 1 LONDON, WEDNESDAY, JUNE 3, 1953

SWEET RATIONING ENDS

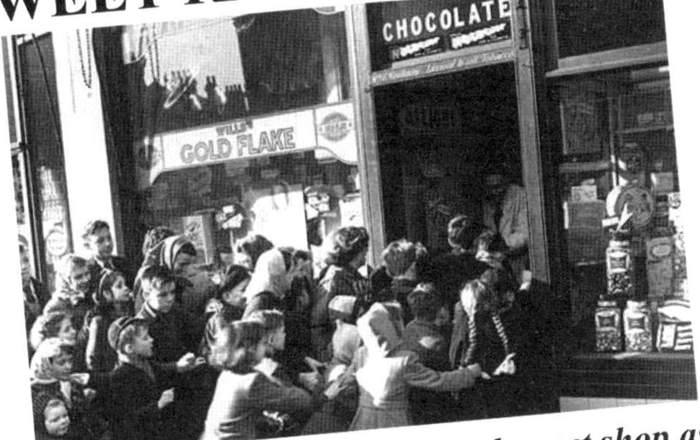

Children heading for their local sweet shop as the first unrationed sweets go on sale

TOFFEE APPLES ARE THE TOP SELLERS, BUT NOUGAT AND LIQUORICE STRIPS ARE GOING FAST!

The government and manufacturers are keen to reassure the public that there will be no repeat of the first attempt to de-ration sweets (April 1949) when suppliers could not keep up with demand and they were put back on ration after four months.

The Daily News

No.2, JULY 21, 1969

MAN LANDS ON THE MOON

Apollo 11 and her crew on the surface of the Moon

NEIL ARMSTRONG IS THE FIRST MAN TO WALK ON THE MOON

The lunar module landed safely at 20.17 GMT. As Armstrong stepped out of the craft, he declared: "That's one small step for man, one giant leap for mankind."

Armstrong described the surface of the Moon as being like powdered charcoal.

5 | Food I

Level A

Materials needed:
- Real food items from the cupboard / fridge (e.g. fruit, vegetables, confectionary, spices, herbs)
- plate, cutlery, napkins (optional).

Use food items you already have at home, or purchase some foods that are new to you to discuss and taste.

Things to think about…
- Taste, texture, smell
- Guess their country of origin
- Which do you prefer? Are there any you don't like?
- Has food, and the way we think about it changed over the years? (e.g. war time rations, modern excessive consumption)

Level B

Materials needed:
- Images of food items (see opposite) or real food items (optional).

Think of ways to group the items to create different dishes. See how many you can come up with!

Suggestions…
- Match images / real foods together to create recipes (e.g. flour, sugar and eggs can be used to make pancakes)
- Which foods go well together? And which don't?
- Which foods are healthy or unhealthy?
- Can you group the foods into different categories e.g. dairy, vegetables, green foods? Or by colour, texture or shape?
- Are there any ingredients you particularly like or dislike in the selection?
- Do you enjoy cooking? Why, or why not?
- Meals (i.e. would you serve this item for breakfast?)

Food activity images

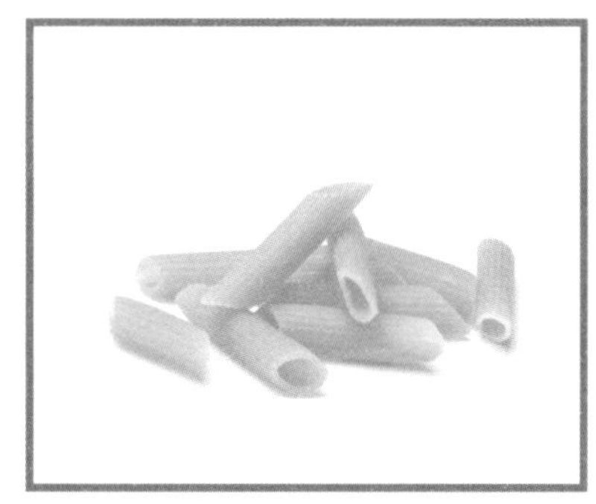

6 | Food II

Level A

Materials needed:
- World cuisine images (below and opposite).

Discuss the images of food using the suggested questions or some of your own.

Things to think about...
- Have you ever tried the foods shown?
- Do any of the foods look similar? Why?
- Have your food preferences changed over the years?
- Do you enjoy trying new foods?
- Can you guess any of the ingredients in the dishes?
- From which countries do you think these foods come from?

Level B

Materials needed:
- Pen and paper (optional)
- timer (optional).

Choose a type of food, and see how many examples you can think of. Perhaps set a timer to make the game more challenging.

Suggestions...
- Soups
- Vegetables
- Foods of a certain colour (e.g. green, orange)
- Fish
- Foods beginning with certain letters (e.g. B – burger, banana, beans etc.)

Food II | 6

7 | Being Creative I

Level A & Level B

Spend the session engaging in a creative activity together.

You may want to consider some of the activities below depending on what materials you have available or what interests you and the person share…

- Baking, cake decorating, cooking
- Knitting, sewing, embroidering, cross-stitch
- Gardening (planting, watering, hanging baskets, herb gardens, window boxes, vegetable patches)
- Painting, drawing (paper, canvas, pot, plates etc.)
- Card making
- Music
- Singing

or you may have plenty of ideas of your own!

Being Creative II | 8

Level A & Level B

Continue with the Being Creative activity you started in session 7 or choose another.

Suggestions...

- Photo frame making, photography, photo collage
- Poems, short stories
- Flower arranging
- Model making (clay, plasticine)
- Patchwork quilt making
- Dancing

9 | Number Games I

Level A

Materials needed:

- Price matching activity (on these pages)

Match the items shown opposite with the prices provided in the table below. You could also gather together some items from the house and guess their prices, or arrange them in order from least to most expensive. The purpose of the activity is to discuss why you and the person have selected the price for each of the products.

Things to think about…

- How much would you pay for these items?
- Would the price for these items be different 20, 40, or 50 years ago?
- Do you think the quality of an item is related to how expensive it is?

Level B

Materials needed:

- Pack of cards, dominoes or any other number games you may have at home (see list below).

Play a number game that requires recognition and use of numbers. Play together or against each other.

Suggestions…

- Card games e.g. Snap!, Pontoon
- Guess whether the next card in the deck will have a higher or lower value
- Bingo
- Dominoes

Price matching

Price	Product Letter	Price	Product Letter
£0.50		£10.00	
£1.19		£20.00	
£2.00		£300.00	
£5.00		£10,000.00	
£7.99		£250,000.00	

Number Games I | 9

10 | Number Games II

Level A

Materials needed:
- Pack of cards, dominoes or any other number games you may have at home
- pen and paper (optional).

Think of games that require recognition and use of numbers. Play together or against each other.

Suggestions…
- Ludo
- Connect 4
- Yahtzee
- Noughts and Crosses

Alternatively…
- Guess how many items in a container e.g. chocolates in a box, pennies in a jar, count them and see whose guess was closest.

Level B

Materials needed:
- Dots and boxes (see opposite).

Play the dots and boxes game provided. Starting with the empty grid of dots, players take turns adding a single horizontal or vertical line between two dots. A player who completes the fourth side of a 1x1 box can claim the square and write the first letter of their name inside it.

Once all of the possible horizontal and vertical lines in the grid have been drawn, count the number of squares for each player. The player with the most squares wins.

Tip
It will be helpful to use two different coloured pens for this activity so that it is easy to identify each player's boxes.

Example dots game in progress

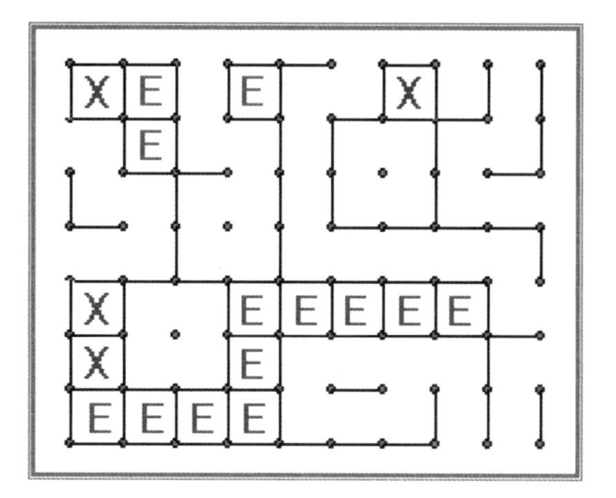

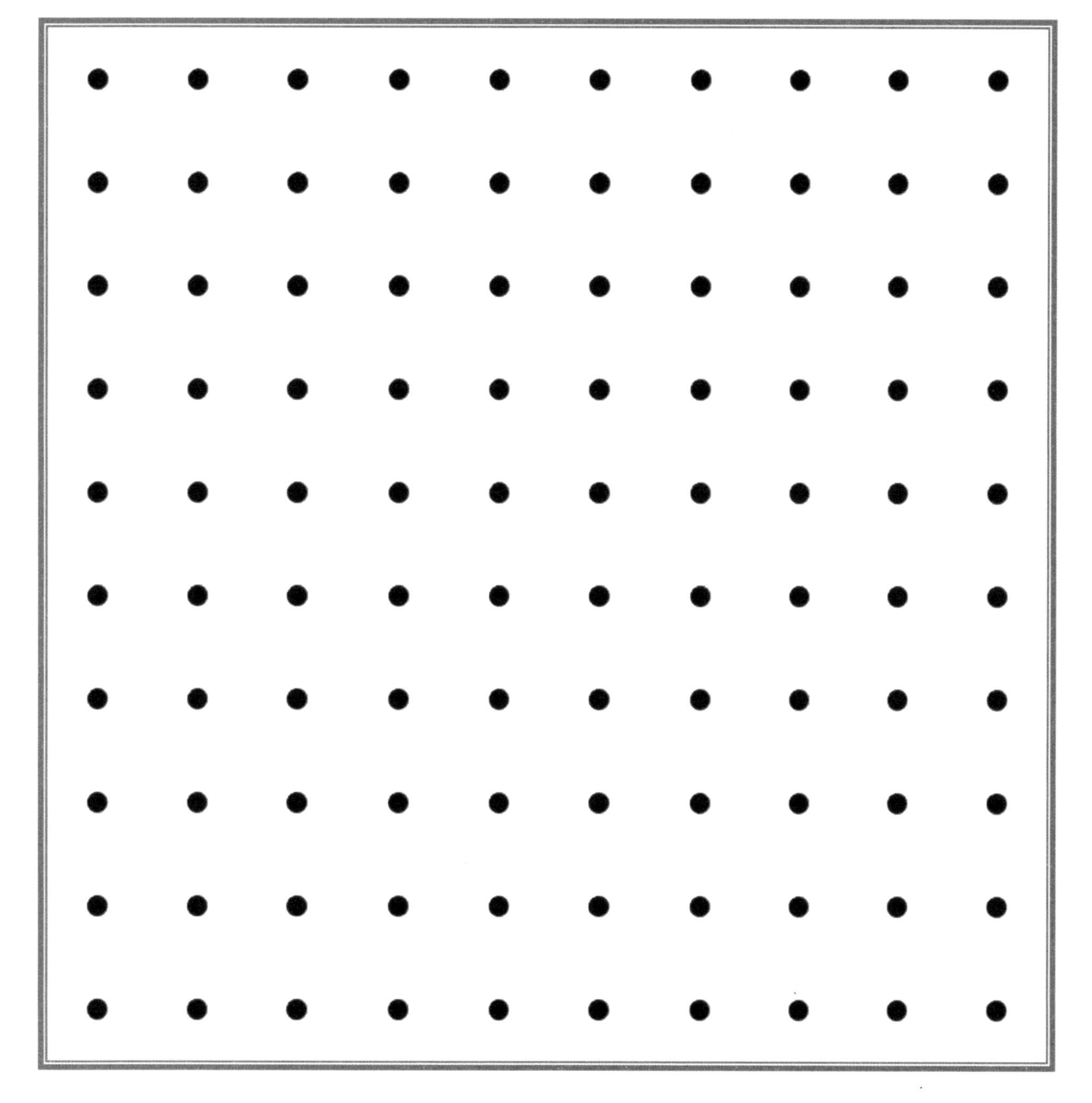

11 | Quiz Games I

Level A

Materials needed:

- Old Wives' Tales Quiz (see opposite).

Discuss whether you think the old wives' tales are true or false. This activity is an opportunity to explore ideas, and perhaps recall some fond memories! The answers have been provided on page 150 if you would like to check these after the session, but you do not need to focus on getting each answer correct.

Things to think about...

- Do you think any of the old wives' tales could be true?
- Have you told any of these tales before? Or have you heard these tales from family members?
- Why do you think we have old wives' tales?
- Where do you think these tales came from?

Level B

Materials needed:

- General Knowledge Quiz (pages 36-39)
- pen, paper (optional).

See if you can guess the answers to the questions in the General Knowledge Quiz. You can mark your answers on a piece of paper or on the activity sheet. Don't worry about your score, this is just for fun!

Try to incorporate discussion into the quiz. For instance, if there is a question about a famous landmark, you could talk about whether you have ever visited the famous landmark or whether you would like to. If any questions are particularly challenging, you can move on. Answers on p150.

Old Wives' Tales Quiz: True or false?

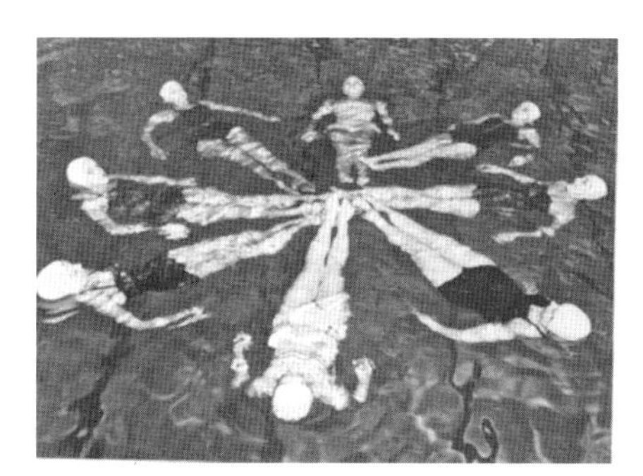

Eating before you swim causes cramp

Sitting too close to the television will ruin your eyes

Carrots are good for your eyesight

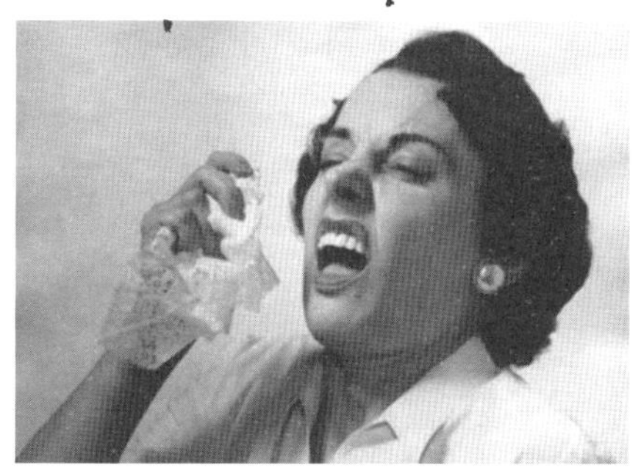

You will catch a cold if you go out on a chilly night with wet hair

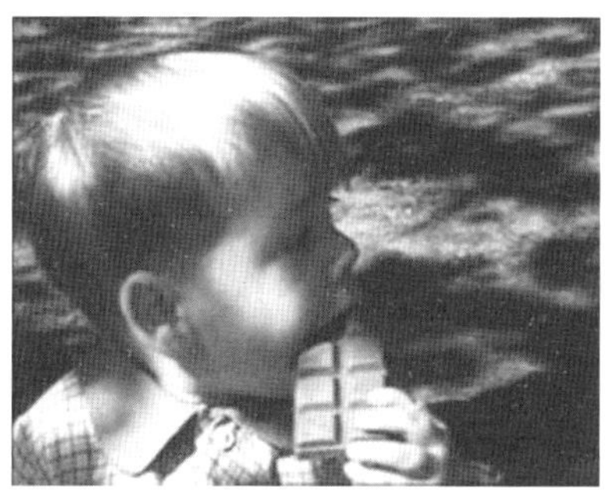

Sugar makes children hyperactive

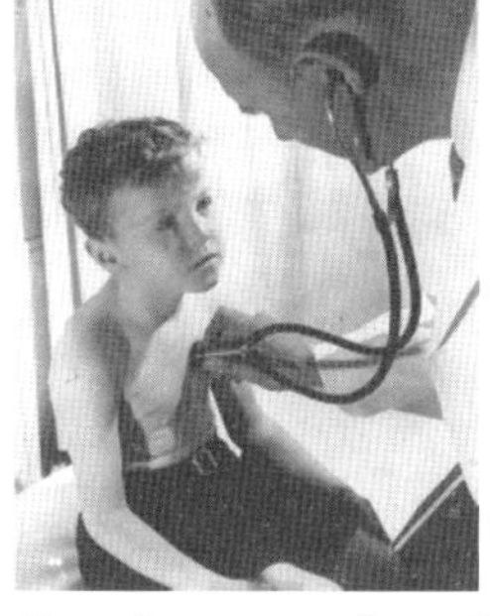

An apple a day keeps the doctor away

Lightning never strikes twice in the same place

Gain a child, lose a tooth

11 | Quiz Games I

General Knowledge Quiz

Primrose, Gladiolus and Foxglove are all types of what?

a) Vegetable

b) Animal

c) Flower

What is the largest land-dwelling animal?

a) Rhinoceros

b) Elephant

c) Giraffe

Which of these landmarks is in New York?

a) Eiffel Tower

b) Statue of Liberty

c) Pyramids

General Knowledge Quiz (continued)

What colour is a ruby?

a) Red

b) Blue

c) Green

What is the name of the world's longest running soap opera?

a) Coronation Street

b) Eastenders

c) Emmerdale

Which of the following is not one of the Seven Deadly Sins?

a) Cleanliness

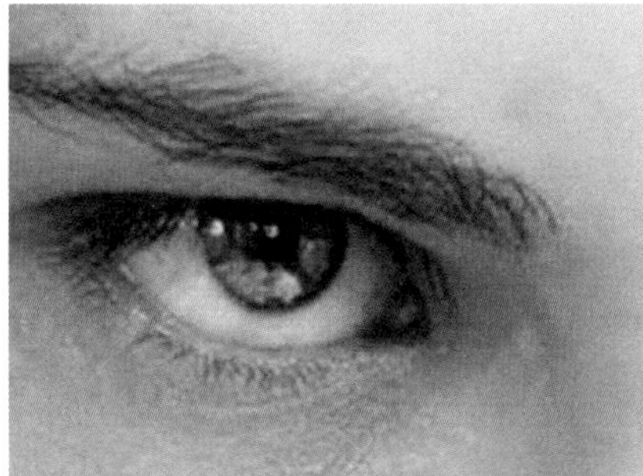
b) Envy

c) Vanity

11 | Quiz Games I

General Knowledge Quiz (continued)

A cat is said to have how many lives?

1	6	9
a) One	**b) Six**	**c) Nine**

Who is married to the Queen of England, Elizabeth II?

a) Prince Charles

b) Prince Philip

c) Prince William

What 'R' is a sport performed on water?

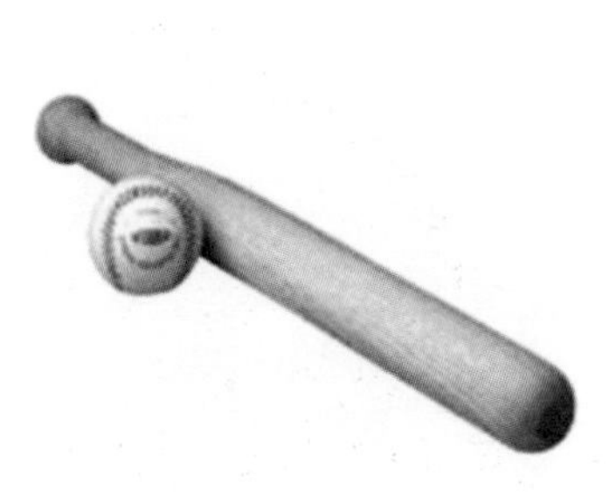

a) Rounders

b) Roller skating

c) Rowing

General Knowledge Quiz (continued)

What is a tsunami?

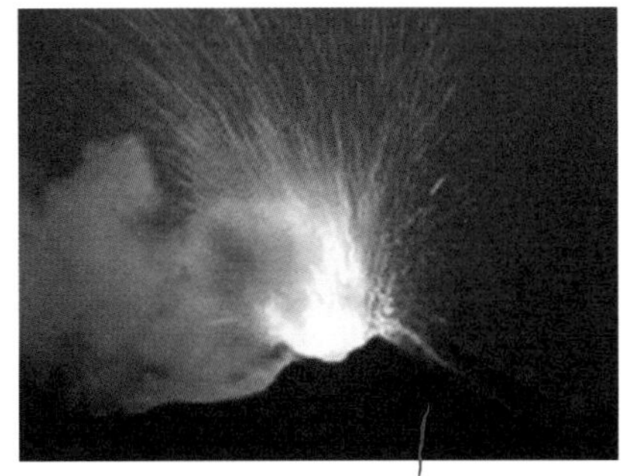
a) A volcanic eruption

b) A giant wave

c) An earthquake

What type of bird do they keep at the Tower of London?

a) Eagle

b) Magpie

c) Raven

What is a 'Penny Black'?

a) Black cab

b) Stamp

c) Bicycle

12 | Quiz Games II

Level A

Materials needed:
- Pen and paper (optional)
- board games (optional).

Play a game you both enjoy.

Suggestions…
- Guess what I'm miming, often known as Charades
- Guess what I'm drawing, often known as Pictionary
- Board games

Perry Como

Glenn Miller

Level B

Materials needed:
- Music Quiz (see this page and opposite)
- pen.

Fill in the missing words from the famous lyrics and match the artist with their song. You might prefer to guess the song title, or just have a discussion about music.

Nat King Cole

Suggestions…
- Sing the song or listen to a record to help you fill in the blanks in the lyrics
- Match the artist with their song title or think of other songs they have released
- Discuss the songs and artists and any fond memories you may have of them.

Vera Lynn

Roy Orbison

You can write your answers on the activity sheet, on a separate piece of paper, or you can sing or discuss the answers. As with all of the iCST activities, try not to focus on the 'correct' answer. If you are finding a question particularly challenging or if you are not familiar with the song, you can move on. Answers are provided on page 151.

Don't sit under the _______ tree with anyone else but me, _______ else but me,
Don't _______ under the _______ tree with anyone else but me, till I come _______ home.

I have often walked down this _______ before,
But the _______ always stayed beneath my feet before.
All at once am I several _______ high.
Knowing I'm on the _______ where you _______.

We'll meet again, don't know _______, don't know _______
But I know we'll meet again some _______ day.
Keep _______ through, just like you always do,
Till the blue _______ drive the dark clouds far away.

Oh every time it _______, it rains _______ from heaven,
Don't you know each _______ contains _______ from heaven.

I've got you under my _______ I've got you _______ in the heart of me,
So deep in my heart that you're really a _______ of me,
I've got you _______ my _______.

She wrote upon it: Return to _______, address unknown. No such _______ ,no such zone.
We had a quarrel, a lover's spat I write I'm sorry but my letter keeps _______ _______.

Pretty _______, walking down the street, Pretty _______ , the kind I _______ to meet,
Pretty _______, I don't believe you, you're not the _______ ,
No one could look as _______ as you.

Magic _______, When two hearts are carin', Magic _______, _______ we've been sharin'
I'll never _______ the moment we kissed, The _______ of the hayride.
The way that we hugged to try to keep warm, While takin' a sleigh _______

When I was just a _______ girl, I asked my _______ ,What will I be?
Will I be _______ ,Will I be rich? Here's what she said to me:
Que _______ , _______ Whatever will be, will be
The _______ not ours, to see. Que sera, sera, What will be, _______ _______.

You're _______ till somebody _______ you, You're nobody till somebody _______
You may be king, you may possess the world and it's _______ ,
But gold won't bring you _______ when you're growing old.

Dean Martin

Doris Day

Bing Crosby

Elvis Presley

Frank Sinatra

13 | Sounds I

Level A

Materials needed:
- Sounds activity sheet (see opposite).

Use the images on the activity sheet provided to stimulate discussion about sounds.

Things to think about...
- Which sounds are pleasant?
- Which sounds are unpleasant?
- Where might you expect to hear these sounds?
- Can you categorise the sounds (i.e. animals, outdoor sounds)?
- Do any of these sounds bring back any memories?

Level B

Materials needed:
- Sound effects (audio section on iCST DVD supplied with this book)
- sounds activity sheet (see opposite)
- pen (optional).

Listen to the clips of sound effects in the audio section on the DVD provided and try to match these with the images on the activity sheet. You can cross the picture off, or place a counter or coin over the picture when you think you've heard its corresponding sound.

Things to think about...
- What do you think the sound is or where might you hear it?
- Is it a pleasant or unpleasant sound?
- Does the sound remind you of anything?

Tips
- You might need to play each track more than once to identify the sounds.
- This activity is focused on interpretation and what each track 'sounds like' rather than responding correctly to each answer. If you would like to check the answers after the session, turn to page 151.
- If you would like to make this activity more challenging, try to guess the sounds without the use of the activity sheet.

Sounds I | 13

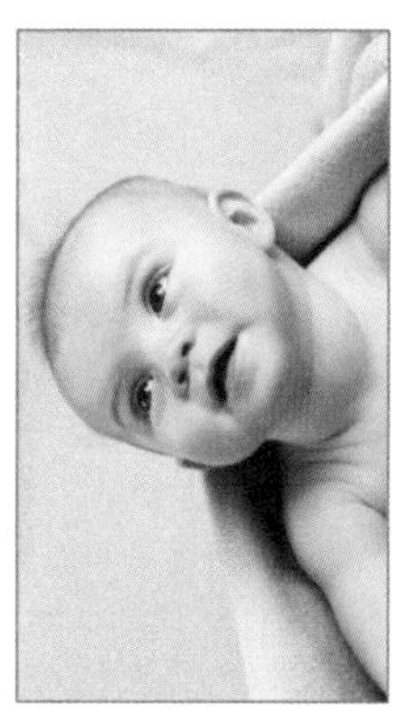
Baby Cooing

Telephone Ringing

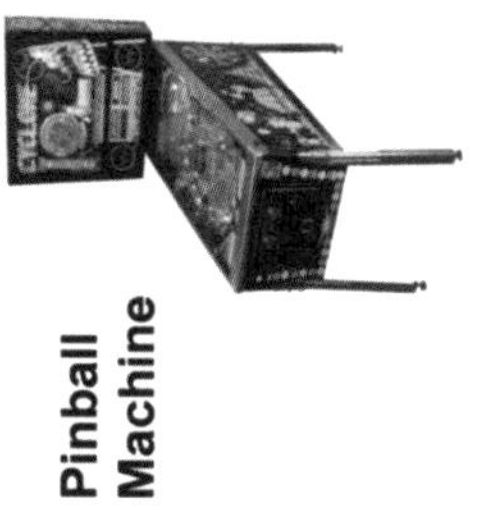
Pinball Machine

Ducks

Train Whistling

Horse Neighing

Birdsong

Cash Register

Cat Meowing

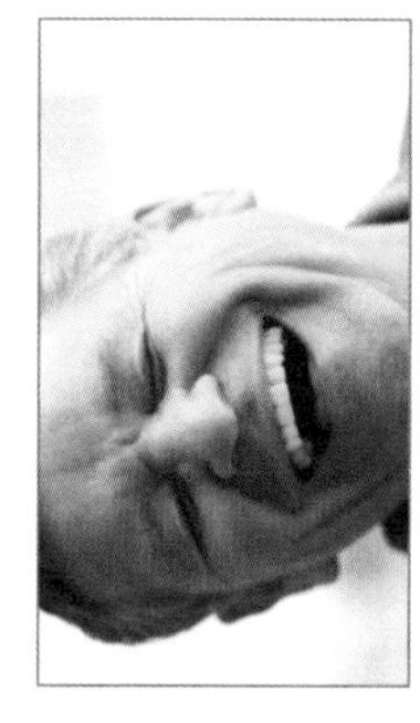
Laughter

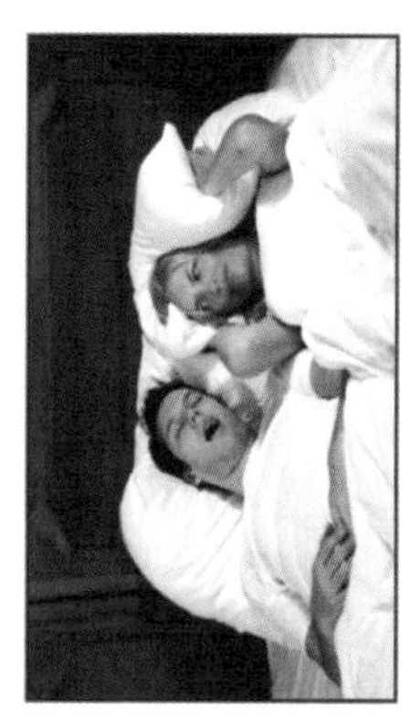
Snoring

Church Bell

Cuckoo Clock

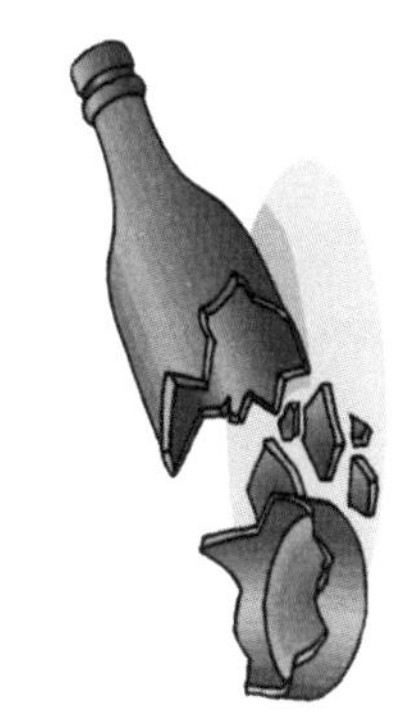
Breaking Glass

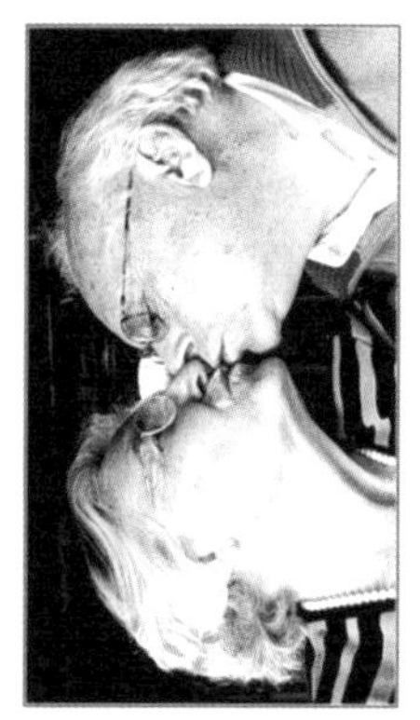
Squeaky Kiss

Fly Buzzing

14 | Sounds II

Level A

Materials needed:

- Styles of music clips (audio section on iCST DVD supplied with this book)
- pen (optional).

Listen to the clips of music on the iCST DVD, and have a discussion about them.

Things to think about…

- What do you think of the music you hear?
- Does the music remind you of anything?
- Where might you hear this music?
- Can you play any musical instruments or would you have liked to learn?
- What styles of music do you like?

Level B

Materials needed:

- Styles of music clips (audio section on iCST DVD supplied with this book)
- styles of music activity sheet (see opposite)
- pen (optional).

Listen to the clips of music on the iCST DVD provided and try to match these with the styles on the activity sheet. Use the topics provided above to generate discussion.

Tips

- You might need to play each track more than once to identify the styles of music.
- This activity is focused on interpretation and what each piece of music 'sounds like'. However, if you would like to check the answers after the session, turn to page 152.
- Try to incorporate discussion into the activity. For example, you could discuss how pleasant or unpleasant the pieces of music are, why you think they belong in each style category, or what sort of music you enjoy listening to.

Styles of Music Activity

CLASSICAL	BLUES	COUNTRY
WALTZ		WORLD
ROCK		REGGAE
FUNK	SALSA	JAZZ

15 | Physical Games I

Level A & Level B

Materials needed:

- Any games or sports equipment you have around the house (optional).

Spend the session playing a physical game. Some suggestions for activities have been provided below.

Suggestions...

- See how long you can keep a balloon in the air for.
- Make a bowling alley with plastic bottles or objects and a ball and see how many you can knock down.
- DIY throwing game: collect together some objects from around the house such as cups, bowls, pans etc. to use as 'goals', and a ball (i.e. ping pong ball). Place the objects at a reasonable distance and see if you can throw the ball into your 'goals'.

These activities can be done standing up or sitting down depending on the physical abilities of the person.

Please make sure you have enough space to do the physical activity you choose, and take care to make the area safe to avoid any accidents.

If you and the person prefer not to engage in a physical game, you can choose an activity you have found enjoyable in previous sessions.

Physical Games II | 16

Level A & Level B

Materials needed:

- Any games or sports equipment you have around the house such as skittles (optional).

Continue with the physical games activity you started in the last session, or choose another physical game or activity to do:

Suggestions…

- Go for a walk in your area or a nearby park. Discuss things you see, hear and smell as you go.
- Have a go at some indoor exercises or stretches, but take care to warm up and cool down.
- Dance to your favourite song or music
- Gardening and tending to indoor plants.

Please make sure you have enough space to do the physical activity you choose, and take care to make the area safe to avoid any accidents.

17 | Categorising Objects I

Level A

Materials needed:

- Pen and paper (optional).

Think of categories and list as many examples as you can in each category. For example, if you chose 'fruit' as a category, you might list apples, pears, oranges, grapes etc.

Suggestions...

- Things you might find in the kitchen, garden, bathroom etc.
- Countries
- Girls' / boys' names
- Famous landmarks
- Colours
- Famous novels

Level B

Materials needed:

- Pen and paper (optional).

You can make the categories game above more challenging by setting a timer. See how many examples you can come up with in the time set. You could also think of more specific categories, such as those shown below.

Suggestions...

- Countries beginning with the letter 'A'
- Famous landmarks in London
- Foods from Italy

Categorising Objects II | 18

Level A

Materials needed:
- Odd one out series (see pages 50 to 53)
- pen (optional).

Choose a selection of the odd one out series to discuss. Choose a selection of series that you think will be most interesting for the person.

Things to think about...
- What are the differences between the items?
- What are the similarities?
- Can you find more than one association between the items?
- Which images do you prefer or dislike?

Level B

Materials needed:
- Odd one out series (see pages 50 to 53)
- pen (optional).

Discuss the items in each odd one out series. Try some of the more challenging series, such as the number or concept cards.

Tips
- Discuss reasons for your answers and see how many differences, similarities and connections you can think of between the items in each series.
- There are many possible answers to this activity. Some of these answers can be found on page 152.

18 | Categorising Objects II

Odd one out series: visual

Categorising Objects II | 18

Odd one out series: visual

18 | Categorising Objects II

Odd one out series: number

5	15
11	225

Odd one out series: concept

Monsoon	Tornado
Hurricane	Typhoon

Odd one out series: concept

Love	**Greed**
Anger	**Hate**

Daisy	**Daffodil**
Dandelion	**Crocus**

19 | Household Treasures I

Level A

Materials needed:

- Images of old and new objects (see pages 55 and 56) or old and new objects that you have at home (e.g. CDs / records, electric whisk / hand held whisk).

Compare and discuss the images or real objects using the following questions as a starting point:

Things to think about…

- What are the objects?
- What are the similarities and differences between the objects?
- Which do you prefer?
- Have you ever owned items like these?
- Which look easier to use?
- Which would be more expensive?

Level B

Materials needed:

- images of old and new objects (see pages 55 and 56)
- pen (optional).

Match the images of old objects with their more modern counterparts. You could draw lines between images to indicate pairs. Use the suggested topics provided above to prompt discussion about the items once you have matched them together.

Household Treasures I | 19

19 | Household Treasures I

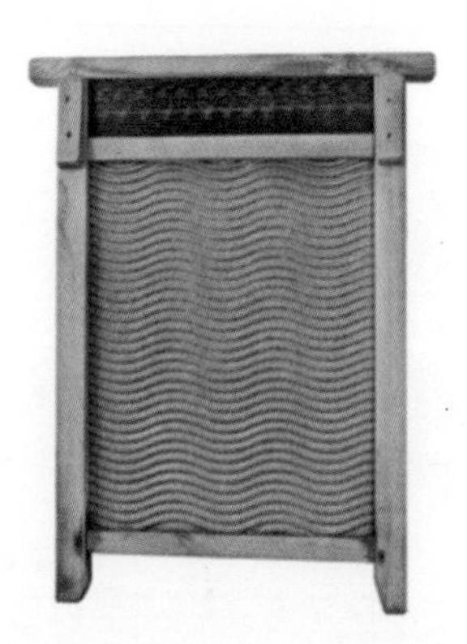

Household Treasures II | 20

Level A

Materials needed:
- Household objects (e.g. telephone, radio)
- pen and paper (optional).

Gather some household items together, or make a list. Discuss the questions below, or come up with questions of your own.

Things to think about...
- Which have the most sentimental value? How about monetary value?
- Which couldn't you live without?
- Did you have any of these objects when you were a child? (e.g. television is a relatively new invention)
- What is the history of each object?
- Is it a family heirloom?
- Is there a particular story attached to it?
- Can you rate the objects in order of importance?

Level B

Think of objects from around the house and try to describe them. You could also mime how the objects are used, and try to guess each object being described from the clues you are given. For example, 'TV' might be described as 'something you would put in the living room', 'something that entertains the family', 'something with an aerial'.

21 | Useful Tips I

Level A & Level B

Materials needed:
- Useful household tips activity sheet (see opposite)
- pen (optional)

Match the household problems with their solutions. You could draw lines between the problems and solutions to indicate pairs. Use the suggested topics provided below to prompt discussion during the activity. As with all iCST activities, the emphasis is on discussing opinions rather than getting the 'right' answer, but we've provided some suggested answers on page 152 for your reference.

Things to think about...
- Do you think the solution would work?
- Have you ever had any of these problems or used any of these solutions?
- Who might encounter these problems?
- Have you tried and tested any solutions of your own to these problems?
- Has the way people deal with problems like these changed over the years?
- Why, or why not?

To stop a door from squeaking...

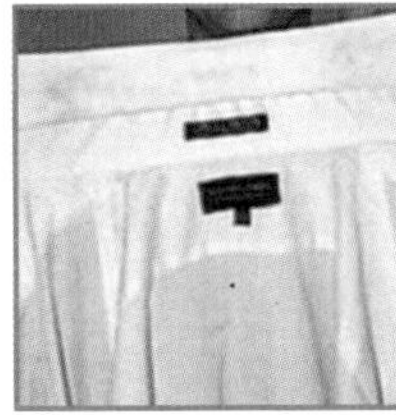

To remove a dirty ring around a shirt collar...

To make threading a needle easier...

To cure a headache...

To prevent new patent leather shoes from cracking...

To kill and repel bedbugs...

To prevent potatoes from sprouting...

To soothe a sore throat...

... place an apple in the bag with them.

... rub with vaseline.

... apply hairspray to the thread. When it is dry it will stiffen enough to pass easily through the eye.

... apply shampoo to the area.

... apply bacon dripping to the area.

... take some honey.

... use a non-stick cooking spray to grease the hinges.

... cut a lime in half and rub it on your forehead.

22 | Useful Tips II

Materials needed:
- Pen and paper (optional).

Level A

Try to come up with solutions to common problems, for example:

- How to get a good night's sleep
- Ways of making new friends
- How to feed a family on a budget
- Ways to stop a baby crying

Level B

What advice would you give to the following people?

- A newly married couple
- A person starting his/her own business
- A person travelling abroad
- A new mother / father
- A person trying to lose weight / live a healthier lifestyle
- A person moving house

Is your advice based on your own experience or someone else's?

Thinking Cards I & II | 23/4

Part I: Level A & Level B

Materials needed:

- Thinking Cards (see pages 62-63).

Choose a selection of the questions and topics provided in the grid, and use these as a guide to generate and encourage discussion. Think creatively and have fun exploring the ideas you come up with together. You should leave enough questions for the next session (below), which is also a thinking cards activity.

If you think of any questions of your own, incorporate these into the activity.

Part II: Level A & Level B

Materials needed:

- Thinking Cards (see pages 62-63).

Continue with the thinking cards activity you began in the last session. Again, choose a selection of the questions from the grid and discuss your thoughts. Perhaps think of a few similar 'thinking questions' of your own.

Tip

- You could throw a coin onto the grid and answer the question the coin lands on.

23/4 | Thinking Cards I & II

If it rained every day for two years, what difference would it make to life in the UK?

If you could invent your perfect day, what would it be like, from start to finish?

If you won the lottery, how would you spend your money?

Would it change your life?

If you were planning a three course meal, what would it be?

If you could create the ideal man / woman, what qualities would you give them?

What animal would best represent you and why?

If you could fly, where would you fly to and why?

If you had to buy 3 gifts for 3 people, who would you buy for, what would you buy, and why?

If you could have three wishes, what would they be?

Imagine you were having a party and could invite anyone you liked, past or present.

Who would you invite? What would they have in common? What would they talk about?

If you could be skilled in one of the following areas, which area would you prefer and how would you use your skill?

Painting Music

Inventing Writing

Imagine you are planning a wedding. List all the things you need to do.

What qualities make a good friend?

If you were Prime Minister for the day, what changes would you make and why?

If you could live in any country in the world, where would you live?

What would your house be like?

"We must value our memories but we must also have a dream."
- *Arthur Fleming*

Come up with a dream or goal for yourself. It may be long or short term.

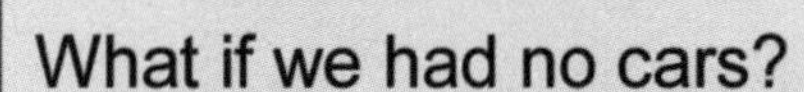

What if we had no cars?

Smells can trigger memories.

Can you think of any smells that remind you of a favourite place or person, or a happy memory?

Are there any smells you find particularly enjoyable?

25 | Visual Clips I

Level A

Materials needed:

- Old and new advertisements activity (see below and opposite)
- pen and paper (optional).

Discuss old and new advertisements.

Things to think about...

- Identify the product being advertised
- Which advert do you prefer for each product and why?
- Which parts of the adverts stand out?
- Do you think these adverts would persuade you to buy the product?
- What are the best and worst features of these adverts?
- Do you think advertising has changed over the years? If so, how?

Level B

Materials needed:

- Old and new advertisements activity (see below and opposite)
- pen and paper (optional).

Discuss old and new advertisements.

Things to think about...

- What is the message behind each advert?
- Which advert do you think is most effective for each product? Why?
- Would any of these adverts influence your opinion about these products?

Alternatively...
Take some advertisements from magazines or newspapers and discuss them using the 'Things to think about...' questions as a starting point.

Tip

- This activity is about comparing, identifying differences and interpretation of themes and ideas.

Visual Clips I | 25

Old and new advertisements

26 | Visual Clips II

Level A

Materials needed:

- Controversial adverts activity sheet (see opposite).

Discuss the controversial advertisements.

Things to think about...

- What do you think the advert is about and how do you feel about the advert?
- Do you think people would be offended by any of the ideas in these adverts?
- Which of the adverts do you think are modern and which are from the past?
- Should any of these adverts be banned?

Level B

Materials needed:

- Controversial adverts activity sheet (see opposite).

Discuss the advertisements using the following suggestions or those from Level A above.

Things to think about...

- What is the message behind each advert?
- Do you think the advert is effective?
- What do you think about using shocking ideas or images in advertising?
- What makes a good advert?

Tips

- You might like to discuss some of the issues highlighted by the adverts and consider whether they should be advertised.
- You may wish to supplement the adverts shown with adverts in magazines, newspapers, internet/television.

The Chef
does everything
but cook
– that's what
wives are for!
I'm giving my wife a
Kenwood Chef
boredpanda.com

You mean a woman can open it?

WIVES.
Look this ad over carefully. Circle the items you want for Christmas. Show it to your husband. If he does not go to the store immediately, cry a little. Not a lot. Just a little. He'll go, he'll go.
Husbands:
Look this ad over carefully. Pick out what you. wife wants. Go buy it. Before she starts to cry.
Dormeyer

For a better start in life
start COLA earlier!
How soon is too soon?
Not soon enough. Laboratory tests over the last few years have proven that babies who start drinking soda during that early formative period have a much higher chance of gaining acceptance and "fitting in" during those awkward pre-teen and teen years. So, do yourself a favor. Do your child a favor. Start them on a strict regimen of sodas and other sugary carbonated beverages right now, for a lifetime of guaranteed happiness.
The Soda Pop Board of America
1515 W. Hart Ave. · Chicago . ILL.

Blow in her face and she'll follow you anywhere.
Tipalet.

Mattel's new M-16 Marauder
If you think this gun looks great, wait'll you hear it!
BRAAP
BRRA-A-A-AP
BRAP
BRAP
WOW! Here's the most authentic-looking and sounding rifle you've ever seen!
Just pull back the cocking lever and this amazing gun is ready to fire. Brap! You can squeeze off single shots. Brra-a-a-ap! Or short bursts.
And listen to this! Keep cocking the fantastic M-16 Marauder and you can cut loose with a solid blast almost a whole minute long! Over 50 rounds! And all with the loud, realistic sound of the actual M-16 rifle!
And another neat thing about Mattel's new M-16 – it doesn't need any caps! No batteries either! You never reload!
So get on target. Get Mattel's new M-16 rifle. It's the greatest!
MATTEL, INC. M TOYMAKERS
See and hear Mattel's M-16 Marauder at your nearest toy store today.

27 | Art Discussion I

Level A

Materials needed:

- Paintings activity (see opposite) or art resources of your own (e.g. history of art books, postcards etc).

Discuss your thoughts and ideas about paintings and works of art.

Things to think about…

- Which of the paintings do you like?
- Would you like to hang any of them on your wall?
- How do the pictures make you feel?

Level B

Materials needed:

- Paintings activity (see opposite) or art resources of your own (e.g. history of art books, postcards etc).

Look at the famous works of art and discuss your thoughts and ideas about them.

Things to think about…

- Can you identify any particular styles of art?
- Do you think the artists who painted these pictures are talented?
- Do you think there is a message behind the painting?

Art Discussion I | 27

28 | Art Discussion II

Level A

Materials needed:

- Different forms of art activity (see opposite).

Discuss the installations and sculptures shown using the discussion points below.

Things to think about...

- What is art?
- Do you consider all of the examples on the activity sheet to be pieces of art?
- Which pieces do you think are worth the most and the least?
- Which pieces do you like and why?
- Are there any you dislike? Why?
- Would you expect to see any of these pieces in a museum or gallery?

Level B

Materials needed:

- Different forms of art activity (see opposite).

Discuss the suggested topics about art listed above in Level A, and the additional topics provided below.

Things to think about...

- Do you think there is a message behind these art pieces?
- Do you think the artist who created the piece is talented?

Alternatively...

Have a go at making your own piece of art. You might want to...

- Create a sculpture out of modelling clay, or create a collage with coloured paper, photographs or images from magazines/catalogues
- Have a go at replicating a famous work of art (e.g. Van Gogh's 'Sunflowers')

Art Discussion II | 28

29 | Faces/Scenes I

Level A & Level B

Materials needed:
- Faces activity sheet (see below and opposite)
- pen and paper (optional).

Discuss the images of faces on the activity sheet using the following points as a guide:

Things to think about…
- Who seems to be the odd one out and why?
- Are the faces linked in any way?
- What can you tell about a person just by looking at their face?
- What sort of character do you think each person has? (e.g. friendly, outgoing etc.)
- What are each face's best / worst features?
- Do any faces stand out to you? Why?
- If you were to choose one as a friend, which would it be and why?
- Who is the most or least attractive?
- How do you think these people are feeling?

You could add to the selection of faces provided images of faces from magazines, newspapers, postcards or books.

Faces/Scenes I | 29

30 | Faces/Scenes II

Level A & Level B

Materials needed:

- Scenes activity (see below and opposite)
- a selection of your own pictures or photographs (optional).

Examine and discuss the landscapes. You could add images from magazines or photos of your own.

Things to think about...

- Similarities and differences between the scenes
- Which landscape do you like best and why?
- Have you ever visited any places like these?
- Would you want to visit any of these places?
- Which scenes look exotic?
- Which scenes look close to home?
- What sort of people might live, work in or visit these places?
- How would you expect to spend your time if you were visiting the place in the picture?
- Would you need to take anything in particular?

Faces/Scenes II | 30

31 | Word Games I

Level A

Materials needed:

- Proverbs word game activity sheet (see opposite)
- pen, paper.

Complete the well known proverbs provided in the activity sheet. Discuss the proverbs as you match them. Answers can be found on page 153. Below are some suggestions to aid your discussion:

Suggestions...

- Discuss the meaning of the proverbs
- Do you think proverbs have any truth in them?
- Have you ever been in a situation where any of these proverbs have applied to you?

Alternatively...

Hangman: Think of a word, film, or song and guess the missing letters. Incorrect letters contribute to the drawing of a 'hangman'

Level B

Materials needed:

- Jumbled letter grid game (see opposite),
- pen, paper (optional).

Find and list as many words as you can find among the random assortment of letters in the grid. Words must be formed from adjoining letters and letters should join in the correct sequence to spell a word. This may be horizontally, vertically, or diagonally, to the left, right, or up-and-down.

Alternatively...

- Words-within-a-word game: think of a long word with lots of different letters (e.g. submarine) and see how many smaller words you can make from it.
- Prefixes game: think of as many words as you can beginning with a common prefix such as PRE-, CON-, PRO-, IN-etc.
- You could set a timer to make the game more challenging.

Proverbs word game

Beauty is only skin

Beggars can't be

Better late than

Better safe than

A friend in need

After a storm

After dinner sit a while

A good beginning makes

Charity begins

History repeats

Home is

Honesty is

Honey catches more flies

A bad workman blames

Once bitten, twice

Damned if you do, damned if you

Every dog has his

Give credit where credit is

Good fences make good

Great minds think alike but

Jumbled letter grid game

A	F	O	P	N
T	O	L	B	A
G	E	T	R	S
M	H	A	U	E
I	T	P	C	E

F	I	M	A	N
N	D	E	R	B
I	G	N	O	W
P	K	L	P	E
A	T	I	Z	A

Qu	A	D	R	U
P	R	E	B	M
U	T	A	O	C
L	I	N	S	S
L	K	W	O	T

S	O	V	B	S
C	O	D	I	M
H	L	E	T	A
I	D	R	W	H
A	M	E	U	C

32 | Word Games II

Level A

Materials needed:

- Pen, paper (optional)
- word puzzles from a magazine or newspaper (optional).

Suggestions...

- Recite the alphabet out loud attaching a word to each letter (e.g. A-ant, B-boy, C- car).
- Rhymes: think of words that rhyme with the following: BALL, TIN, PIG, BARN, BASE, BARE, SOAP.
- Complete a word game from a newspaper together (e.g. crossword, word search).

Level B

Materials needed:

- Word search (see opposite)
- pen, paper (optional).

14 'career' words are hidden in the grid. The aim of the activity is to find as many words as you can. All of the words to find are shown below the grid.

Words may be across, up, down, diagonally and backwards in the grid. You do not need to find all of the words. For reference, after the session, the answers can be found on page 153.

Alternatively...

- Taboo: think of a word for your partner to guess, and try to describe it without using the word itself. Example: If the word is 'dog', you might say 'an animal', 'four legs', 'barks'. You could both write ideas for words on slips of folded paper and put them in a hat.
- Synonyms: think of words that have the same meaning as the following: HAPPY, SAD, CLEVER, BEAUTIFUL, BIG, SMALL.

Z	M	A	N	A	G	E	R	S	U
E	B	A	K	E	R	O	H	E	T
N	T	D	O	C	T	O	R	C	S
G	E	U	S	C	O	P	E	R	I
I	S	T	A	V	E	T	H	E	R
N	R	S	U	P	I	I	C	T	O
E	U	I	I	H	B	C	A	A	L
E	N	T	C	W	H	I	E	R	F
R	C	R	G	E	L	A	T	Y	I
A	A	A	F	L	O	N	J	H	Q

Words to find:

Actor
Architect
Artist
Baker
Chef
Doctor
Engineer
Florist
Manager
Nurse
Optician
Secretary
Teacher
Vet

33 | Slogans I

Level A

Materials needed:

- Product slogans activity (see opposite).

The boxes provided show the names of products and three slogans that have been used in advertising campaigns for each. Discuss the slogans, and choose which best fits each product.

Things to think about…

- Which slogan do you prefer and can you think of any alternative slogans?
- How do you decide which products to buy?
- Does advertising serve a useful purpose?
- What is your favourite slogan?
- Do you think that slogans are more effective on TV, over the radio or in the paper?
- Have you ever bought a product because of the advertisement?

Level B

Materials needed:

- Slogan matching activity (see pages 82-83).

See if you can guess which products the slogans belong to. Draw a line to link the matching slogans and products. Discuss some of the topics suggested above in Level A. The answers to this activity can be found on page 153.

Tip

- If some of these products are unfamiliar, just have a guess if you are unsure or move onto the next product.

Product slogans activity

Alka Seltzer

a) Plop plop, fizz fizz, oh what a relief it is!
b) Try it, you'll like it
c) I can't believe I ate the whole thing!

British Egg Marketing Board

a) Was there a lion on your egg this morning?
b) There is a lion on my egg
c) Go to work on an egg

Butlins

a) Play happy families
b) Come to life. Come to Butlins
c) A million holidays. One Butlins

Daily Mirror

a) Forward with Britain
b) Forward with the people
c) Biggest daily sale on Earth

British Rail

a) Let the train take the strain
b) This is the age of the train
c) We're getting there

33 | Slogans I

Slogan matching activity

The appliance of science

Because life's complicated enough

Does she or doesn't she?

It's the real thing

It's what your right arm's for

Put a tiger in your tank

For mash get smash

They're grrrreat!

The best a man can get

Slogan matching activity

It beats as it sweeps as it cleans

For hands that do dishes

Finger-lickin' good

Because I'm worth it

A Mars a day helps you work rest and play

I liked it so much I bought the company

Let your fingers do the walking

Only the crumbliest, flakiest Chocolate

Snap, crackle and pop

34 | Slogans II

Level A & Level B

Materials needed:

- Matching logos with brands activity (see below and opposite)
- pen (optional).

Match the logo with its associated brand and discuss the logos. Answers on p154.

Things to think about…

- Do you think the logo is a good representation of the brand?
- Do you think having a recognisable logo is important to companies?
- Which logo do you prefer and why?

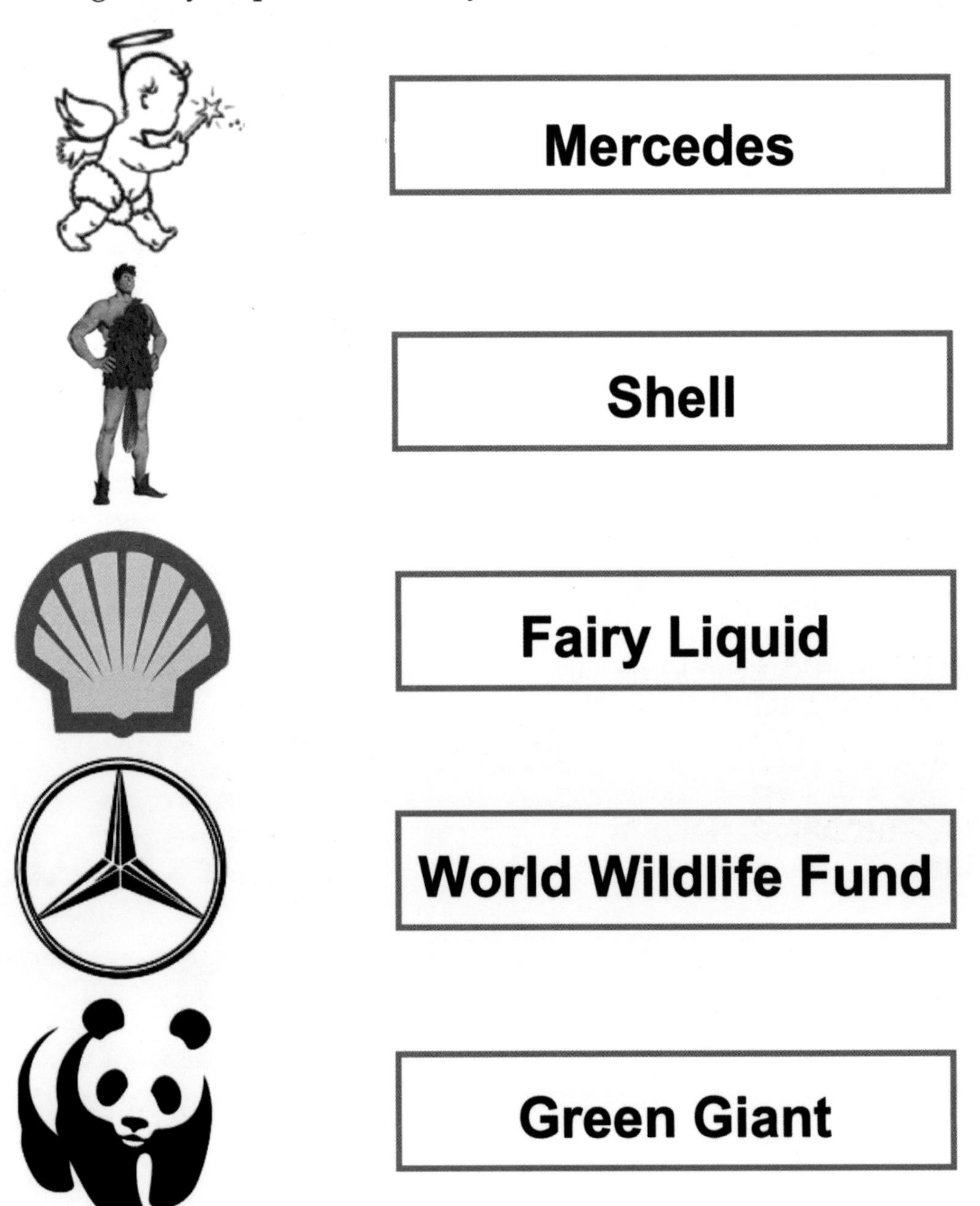

Oxfam

Rolls Royce

YOUR M&S

McDonald's

Penguin Books

Marks and Spencer

35 | Associated Words I

Level A

Materials needed:

- Matching associated pairs activity (see opposite)
- pen and paper (optional).

Think of words associated with the words on the activity sheet.

There might be more than one possible association, so see how many you can think of. Examples of associations can be found on page 154.

You can either discuss your answers or write them on the sheet or on a separate piece of paper. Add pairs of your own if you wish.

Things to think about...

- Can you think of more than one possible answer?
- Can you think of your own pairs?
- Can you imagine one half of the pair without the other?

Level B

Materials needed:

- Pen, paper (optional)
- timer (optional).

Think of a topic such as 'the seaside', 'Christmas', or 'on the farm'. List as many words as you can that you would associate with the chosen topic. You might want to set a time target to make the activity more challenging.

Associated pairs activity

Amounts

Cup of…

Loaf of …

Slice of…

Jug of…

Pint of …

Gallon of…

Reel of…

Ball of…

Pair of …

Bucket of …

Couples

Laurel and…

Morecambe and…

Little and …

Places

Westminster

Buckingham

Windsor

Trafalgar

Piccadilly

Nelson's

Waterloo

Canterbury

Charing

New

Times

Capitol

General

Flora and…

Bed and…

Bow and…

Breaking and…

Cats and…

Chalk and…

Day and…

Heaven and…

Left and…

36 | Associated Words II

Level A

Materials needed:
- Proverbs matching activity (see opposite)
- pen.

Complete the well known proverbs. Discuss the proverbs as you match them. Answers can be found on page 155.

Suggestions...
- What do each of the proverbs mean?
- Do you think proverbs have any truth in them?
- Have you ever been in a situation where any of these proverbs have applied to you?

Level B

Materials needed:
- Proverbs crossword (see opposite)

Have a go at solving the proverbs crossword. Complete the proverbs and enter the missing words in the puzzle grid. Discuss the proverbs as you complete the puzzle. Answers can be found on page 155.

Suggestions...
- What do each of the proverbs mean?
- Are there any times in your life when these proverbs have applied to you?
- Have a go at the proverbs matching activity provided for Level A.

Proverbs activity

A stitch in time

Make hay while

A watched kettle never

The grass is always greener

A bird in the hand is worth

Strike while the iron is

Many hands

Too many cooks

Don't put all your eggs

Absence makes the heart

Out of sight

Don't cry over

Don't cut off your nose

Don't have too many irons

Don't look a gift horse

Be careful what you wish for

Beauty is in the eye

Great oaks from little acorns

A half truth is a whole

He who dares

If at first you don't succeed

Ignorance is

Laughter is the best

Proverbs crossword

1.	2.		3.			
			4.			
	5.					
6.			7.	8.		9.
10.		11.				
		12.				
13.						

ACROSS:

1. The more you get the more you ______
4. Strike while the iron is ______
5. Old habits ______hard
7. Many hands ______light work
10. There's no fool like an ______fool
12. Love conquers ______
13. Do as I ______, not as I do

DOWN:

2. All's fair in love ______war
3. You can't win ______all
6. Barking ______seldom bite
8. ______in a day's work
9. Money is the root of all ______
11. Every dog has his ______

37 | Orientation I

Level A & Level B

Materials needed:
• World map
• UK map
• images from magazines or brochures
• holiday photos
• stickers or pins (optional)
• pen, paper (optional).

Discuss travel and places of interest using world and local maps, images from magazines and brochures, or your own holiday photos.

Things to think about…
• Place of birth
• Places you have visited
• Places you have lived
• Places relatives live, or ancestors came from
• Places you would like to visit and why

If you are using maps, you might like to mark these places with a pin or sticker.

Orientation II | 38

Level A

Materials needed:
- Map or images of local area (optional)
- pen, paper, stickers (optional).

Locate and mark places of interest to you (e.g. your home, favourite park).

Suggestions…
- Identify places of interest on the map (e.g. local library, the post office)
- Talk about how the local area has changed over the years
- Where would you go in your local area to…
  - Buy groceries or clothes
  - Send packages or parcels
  - Have a meal
  - Catch a bus or train.

Level B

Materials needed:
- Pen, paper.

Draw a map of your local town or street.

Suggestions…
- Locate and mark places or areas of interest on the map
- Plan a route from one place to another and think about what you might pass on the way. Are there alternative routes or modes of transport that could be used?

39 | Using Money I

Level A

Materials needed:

- Everyday household items (i.e. bread, milk, toothpaste) or images of everyday products (catalogues, magazines).

Collect household items together (or images from catalogues/magazines). Use the following questions to prompt discussion about the cost of the items. You could write the actual or estimated cost of each item on pieces of paper and try to match these to each item. This is a good activity to do after shopping, using receipts of recently purchased items.

Things to think about…

- How much do you think each item costs?
- Can you organise the items into price order?
- Has the cost of everyday items changed much over the years? If so, why do you think this might be?

Level B

Materials needed:

- I'll pay with my… activity sheet (see opposite)
- pen.

Discuss which method of payment you would choose to pay for the items on the activity sheet, giving reasons for your choices.

Things to think about…

- How much does the item cost?
- Are more than one of these payment types applicable?
- How much would you be prepared to pay for the item?

Tips

You can circle or tick the payment you would choose for each of the items on the activity sheet. This activity is focused on your personal opinions and preferences. You may give more than one answer for each option.

A holiday	A chocolate bar	An electricity bill
Credit Card	Credit Card	Credit Card
Cheque Book	Cheque Book	Cheque Book
Cash (notes)	Cash (notes)	Cash (notes)
Small change	Small change	Small change
Direct debit	Direct debit	Direct debit
Debit Card	Debit Card	Debit Card

A new pair of shoes	A week's worth of shopping	Deposit on a house
Credit Card	Credit Card	Credit Card
Cheque Book	Cheque Book	Cheque Book
Cash (notes)	Cash (notes)	Cash (notes)
Small change	Small change	Small change
Direct debit	Direct debit	Direct debit
Debit Card	Debit Card	Debit Card

40 | Using Money II

Level A

Materials needed:

- Pen and paper (optional)
- any currency you might have, i.e. foreign, old fashioned or modern notes / coins (optional)
- foreign currency activity (see opposite).

Discuss different types of money, such as foreign currency, or old British currency e.g: pounds, shillings, and pence. Below are some ideas for discussion topics:

Things to think about...

- Do you ever use foreign currency? If so, how easy is it to use?
- How do you keep your money safe when on holiday? (UK or abroad)
- What sort of things do you budget for on holiday? (e.g. souvenirs, trips, meals)
- Should every country have the same currency?

If you have any currency, compare and contrast the different types. Talk about where the currency is from, how easy it is to use etc.

Level B

Materials needed:

- Foreign currency activity (see opposite).

Discuss foreign currency. Opposite there are images of notes and coins from different countries for you to use as a reference during your discussion. You can include any real examples of foreign currency you may have in the activity. Answers can be found on page 155.

Things to think about...

- Do you ever use foreign currency? How easy is it to use?
- Should the UK convert from the Pound Sterling to the Euro?
- What do you think of each of the currencies?
- Where do you think they are used? Why? Are there any clues on the notes and coins that can help you guess where they are used?
- Do any of the currencies look similar?

Using Money II | 40

41/2 | Word Games I & II

Level A

Materials needed:
- Word games (from magazines, puzzle books etc.)
- pen, paper
- word based board games (optional).

Below are some suggestions of word games:

- Hangman: Think of a word, film, song title or famous person and draw a number of dashes for each letter of the word / name, and guess the missing letters. Incorrect letters contribute to the drawing of a 'hangman'.
- Complete a word game from a newspaper together (e.g. crossword, word search).
- Taboo: Think of a word for your partner to guess, and try to describe it without using the word itself. If the word were 'dog', you might say 'an animal', or 'barks'.
- Words-within-a-word game: Think of a long word with lots of different letters in (e.g. paleontological) and see how many smaller words you can make from it.

Level B

Materials needed:
- Word games (from magazines, puzzle books etc.)
- pen, paper
- word based board games (optional).

Suggestions...
- Complete a word game from a newspaper together
- Words-within-a-word game: think of a long word with lots of different letters in (e.g. submarine, continental) and see how many smaller words you can make from it.
- Prefixes game: think of as many words as you can beginning with a common prefix such as PRE-, CON-, PRO-, IN-etc.
- Scrabble or any other board-based word games you have.

Word Games II | 42

43 | Art Discussion I

Level A

Materials needed:
- Self portraits activity (see opposite)
- pen and paper (optional)
- scissors (optional).

Discuss your thoughts about the self portraits.

Things to think about...
- What would you consider to be a self portrait? E.g. painting, photograph etc.
- Why do you think artists create self portraits?
- Do any of the portraits shown stand out to you? Why?
- Can you tell anything about the artist from their portrait?
- Do you think the self portrait looks like the artist who created it?

Level B

Materials needed:
- Self portraits activity (see opposite)
- pen and paper (optional)
- scissors (optional).

See if you can match each self portrait with the artist. Use the topics in Level A to stimulate discussion about the images and artists.

This activity is not focused on identifying the artists shown, but their names can be found on page 155.

Self portraits

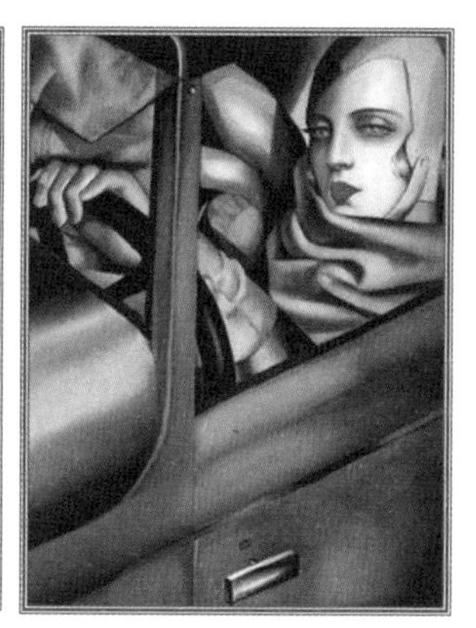

Artists

44 | Art Discussion II

Level A

Materials needed:
- Architecture activity (see below and opposite)
- pen and paper (optional).

Discuss your thoughts about the buildings.

Things to think about...
- Do you think a building can be a form of art?
- Do you think any of the buildings are beautiful?
- Which of the buildings do you think are old, and which are modern?
- Is there anything about each building that stands out to you?
- What styles of building do you like?
- What do you think each building is used for?

Level B

Materials needed:
- Architecture activity (see below and opposite)
- pen and paper (optional).

Discuss your thoughts about the buildings. Which of the following categories would you put each building into?

- Office building
- Hotel
- Complex with homes, offices and shops
- House
- Visitor attraction
- Concert venue

Discuss why you think each building belongs in each category, using the topics in Level A to stimulate discussion.

Art Discussion II | 44

45 | My Life (Occupations) I

Level A

Materials needed:
- Professions activity (see opposite)
- pen (optional).

See if you can identify the professions shown in the images. Discuss the reasons for your choices. Answers are on page 156

Things to think about.....
- How did you guess the profession?
- Are any of these professions similar to your own?
- If you had to do one of the professions shown, which own would it be and why?
- What did you like most about your own profession? What did you like least?
- Which profession do you think has the highest or lowest wage?

Level B

Materials needed:
- Professions activity (see opposite)
- pen (optional).

See if you can identify the professions shown on the activity sheet. Jot down the 'clues' that helped you guess on the activity sheet. Discuss the following topics as part of the activity:

Things to think about...
- Do you think men and women are seen as equal in the workplace? Why, or why not? Should men be paid more than women or vice versa?
- Are any of these professions similar to your own?
- Have things changed in the workplace over the years? (i.e. safer working conditions, workers' rights, pension schemes)
- When you were at school, did you know which profession you wanted to go into?

My Life (Occupations) I | 45

Occupation:
Clues in the photo:

Occupation:
Clues in the photo:

Occupation:
Clues in the photo:

Occupation:
Clues in the photo:

Occupation:
Clues in the photo:

Occupation:
Clues in the photo:

Occupation:
Clues in the photo:

Occupation:
Clues in the photo:

46 | My Life (Occupations) II

Level A & Level B

Materials needed:
- 'What does it take to be a...?' activity (see opposite)
- pen (optional)

Using the activity sheet, list any items that the professionals might need when they are at work, and any personality traits you think these professionals should have or need to do their job well.

Things to think about...
- What other tools might these people use in their jobs?
- What tools did you use in your profession?
- Can you mime how you would use the different tools?
- Explain how you chose the traits for each profession
- Do you think it is important to have a job you enjoy?
- How important is job salary?

My Life (Occupations) II

'What does it take to be a...?'

Doctor

Traits: re-assuring; talks u thru; Believeable

Tools: Steathascope; Hammer – test reaction – knees; Hands for pulse; Needle for blood test

Teacher

Traits: understanding / hold their attention; Patience; Learn – teach subject; discipline

Tools: Books; Blackboard; Chalk

Plumber

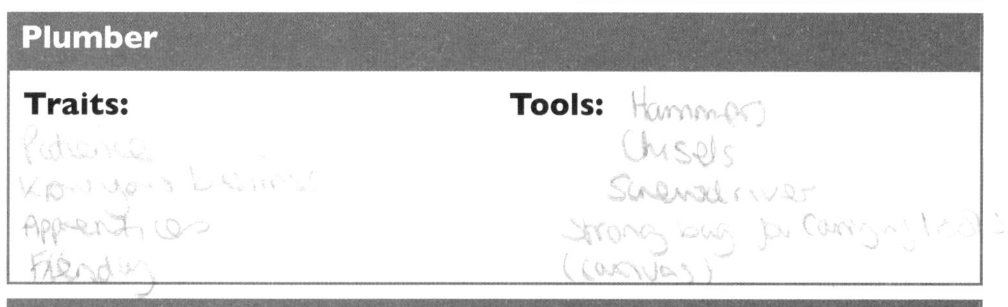

Traits: Patience; Friendly

Tools: Hammers; Chisels; Screwdriver; strong bag for carrying tools (canvas)

Secretary

Traits: Helpful; flexible; friendly

Tools: phone; Notebook

Taxi Driver

Traits: Jovial; Friendly; Sociable; Helpful

Tools: Know where to is going; meter; money

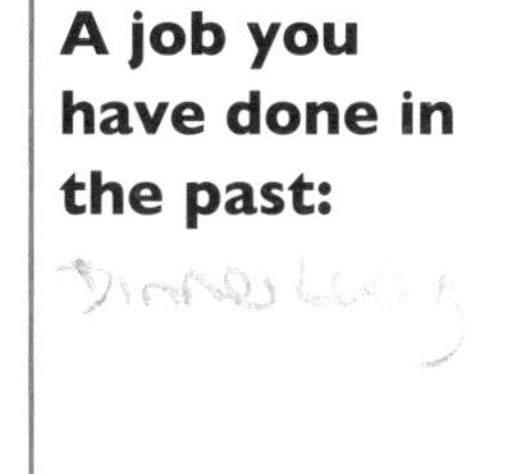

A job you have done in the past:

Traits I needed to have for my job: Patience; Organisational skills

Tools I needed in my job: Notebook; Ring binder!!

47 | Useful Tips I

Level A & Level B

Materials needed:

- Tips for a healthy lifestyle activity (see below)
- pen and paper (optional).

Have a discussion about healthy lifestyles. You may want to complete the 'Tips for a healthy lifestyle' activity sheet below to aid your discussion.

Things to think about…

- What do you consider to be healthy living? Food & Exercise
- Is it important to you to lead a healthy lifestyle? Yes.
- Do you have any tips for eating healthier? Don't eat to much greasy fo
- Do you think it is expensive to maintain a healthy lifestyle? not necessarily
- How do you think society can help people to live a healthier lifestyle? stop some of adverti
- Do you have any tips for living a healthier lifestyle? Walk from 1 stop to another

Tips for a healthy lifestyle activity

Can you think of 5 tips to help you live a healthy lifestyle?

1. More walking
2. Portion Control – Dont load your plate up
3. Eat fresh fruit & vegetables
4.
5.

Can you think of 5 things to avoid if you want to live a healthy lifestyle?

1. eat less fatty food
2. stop smoking
3. excessive drinking
4.
5.

Level A & Level B

Materials needed:

- Pen and paper (optional).

What are your views on the following current issues related to healthy living?

- Childhood obesity
- Smoking in public
- Binge drinking
- Dieting
- Drug use

Things to think about...

- What is the impact of these issues for people and society?
- What are the possible solutions to any problems related to these issues and who should be responsible for providing them?
- Do you have a personal experience related to these aspects of healthy living?
- Are these old or new issues for society?

You might like to include relevant images or news articles in your discussion.

49 | Physical Games I

Level A & Level B

Materials needed:

- Any games or sports equipment you have around the house (optional).

Spend the session playing a physical game. Some suggestions for activities have been provided below.

Suggestions…

- See how long you can keep a balloon in the air for.
- Make a bowling alley with plastic bottles or objects and a ball and see how many you can knock down.
- DIY throwing game: collect together some objects from around the house such as cups, bowls, pans etc. to use as 'goals', and a ball (i.e. ping pong ball). Place the objects at a reasonable distance and see if you can throw the ball into your 'goals'.

These activities can be done standing up or sitting down depending on the physical abilities of the person.

Please make sure you have enough space to do the physical activity you choose, and take care to make the area safe to avoid any accidents.

If you and the person prefer not to engage in a physical game, you can choose an activity you have found enjoyable in previous sessions.

Physical Games II | 50

Level A & Level B

Materials needed:

- Any games or sports equipment you have around the house such as skittles (optional).

Continue with the physical games activity you started in the last session, or choose another physical game or activity to do:

Suggestions…

- Go for a walk in your area or a nearby park. Discuss things you see, hear and smell as you go.
- Have a go at some indoor exercises or stretches, but take care to warm up and cool down.
- Dance to your favourite song or music
- Gardening and tending to indoor plants.

Please make sure you have enough space to do the physical activity you choose, and take care to make the area safe to avoid any accidents.

51 | Sounds I

Level A & Level B

Materials needed:

- Musical Instruments clips (audio section on iCST DVD supplied with this book)
- musical instruments activity sheet (see opposite)
- pen and paper (optional).

Listen to the clips on the DVD and try to identify the musical instruments you can hear. Discuss topics related to music and musical instruments.

Things to discuss…

- Have you ever played a musical instrument?
- Which musical instruments do you like the sound of?
- Which instruments do you dislike the sound of?
- Do you associate any musical instruments to any particular styles of music?

Alternatively…

If you have any musical instruments (i.e. percussion instruments) you could play along to familiar music.

Tips

- You might need to play each track more than once to identify the musical instruments. You can cross the image of the musical instrument off when you hear it.
- This activity is focused on interpretation and what you think each track 'sounds like'. Don't worry too much about getting each answer correct, but if you'd like to have a look at the answers they're on page 156.

FLUTE

DRUMS

GUITAR

TRIANGLE

PIANO

BASS

XYLOPHONE

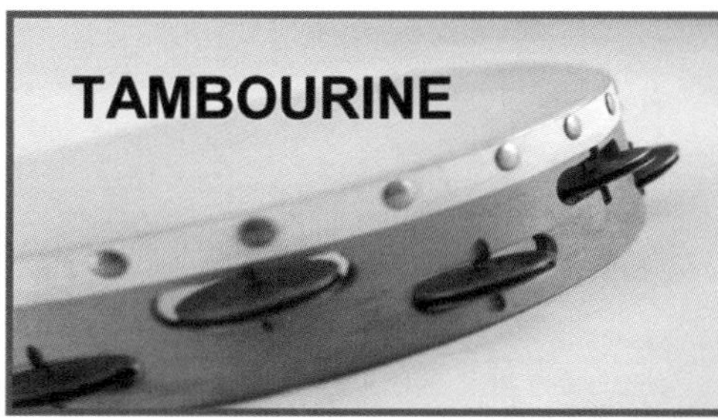
TAMBOURINE

TRUMPET

ORGAN

52 | Sounds II

Level A & Level B

Materials needed:

• Pen and paper (optional),.

Think of places and list sounds you might expect to hear if you were there. For example, at the seaside you might hear the sound of the waves on the beach, children playing, sea gulls etc.

Suggestions…

• At the seaside
• In a restaurant
• In the kitchen
• In the garden
• In the office
• In the countryside

Alternatively…

You could observe noises and sounds around the house, in the garden or when going out for a walk and discuss what you can hear and where these sounds might be coming from. You might like to discuss the associations we make with certain common sounds (i.e. alarm -waking up).

Sounds II | 52

53 | Childhood I

Level A

Materials needed:

- Childhood toys activity (see opposite)
- pen and paper (optional)
- old or new childhood toys (optional).

Use the images provided or real toys to prompt discussion about childhood toys and games.

Things to think about…

- Which of the toys seems like the most appealing or fun?
- Did you play with any of the toys and games shown as a child?
- Do you think children nowadays play with toys like these?

If you are using real toys, discuss these and demonstrate how you might use them. If you have a selection of old and new toys, compare and contrast them.

Level B

Materials needed:

- Childhood toys activity (see opposite)
- pen and paper (optional)
- old or new childhood toys (optional).

Using the images on the activity sheet, or real toys, generate discussion about childhood toys.

Things to think about…

- Can you identify the toys and games?
- What do you think the rules of each game are?
- Can you group the toys and games into categories? (e.g. games you would play outside)

The names of the toys and games can be found on page 156.

Childhood I | 53

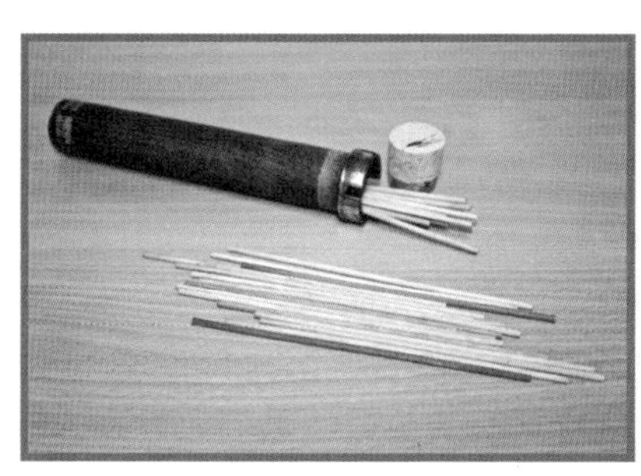

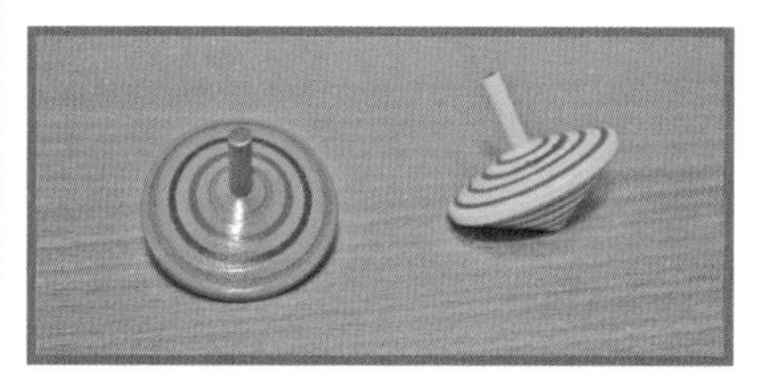

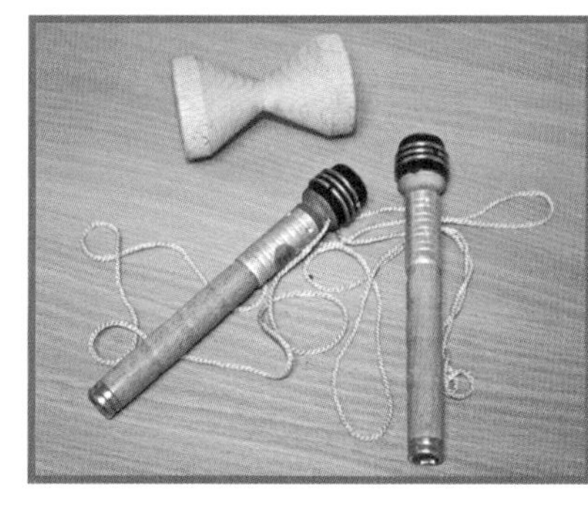

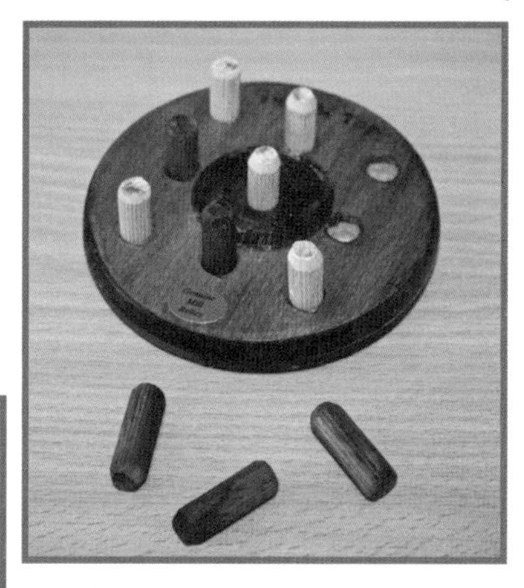

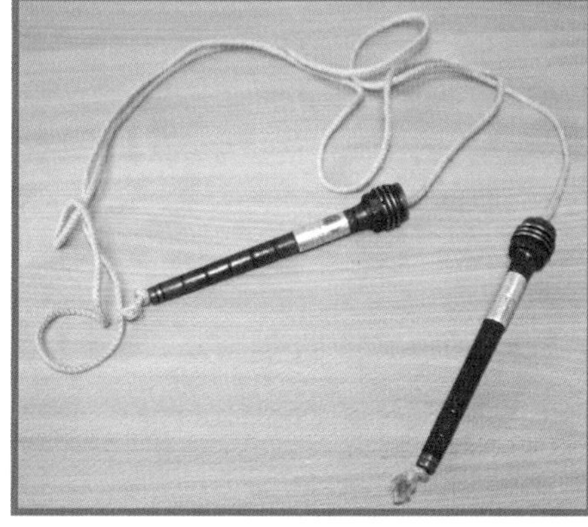

54 | Childhood II

Level A

Materials needed:
- Childhood photos of friends and family.

Look at your childhood photographs alongside those of friends and family members, and have a discussion about them using the following questions as a starting point:

Things to think about...
- What were you like as a child?
- Do the photos have a story behind them?
- Can you see a family resemblance in the photos of your relatives as children?
- What kinds of things did you like to do as a child?
- What was school like?

Level B

Materials needed:
- Pen and paper (optional)
- container (optional).

Have a discussion about your childhood prompted by the following questions:

- What were your favourite hobbies as a child? Did you have any pets?
- Did you have a best friend when you were a child? Where did you play, and which games were your favourite?
- Were you well behaved or mischievous as a child?
- What was the area you grew up in like? How did you get to school when you were a child? Do you have any stories from your childhood?

You could write the questions down on slips of paper, put them in a container and pick them out randomly.

Childhood II | 54

55 | Food I

Level A

Materials needed:

- Dream menu activity (see opposite)
- pen and paper (optional).

Plan your dream meal. Use the activity sheet as a guide to plan your favourite meal.

Things to think about…

- What would you have for each course?
- What would you need in order to prepare it?
- What drinks would you choose to go with the meal?
- If you were having a dinner party, who would you invite, and why?

Level B

Materials needed:

- Menu planning activity (see opposite)
- pen and paper (optional).

Plan the following meals using the ingredients on the activity sheet:

- An evening meal for a family of 4, including at least two types of vegetable
- An evening meal for a vegetarian couple
- A lunch box meal
- A quick meal for a busy person
- A breakfast meal

Things to think about…

- How would you cook each ingredient (i.e. boil, roast) and would you need any extra ingredients?
- How long would each meal take to prepare and cook and how much would each meal cost to make?

Alternatively…

You might like to do some cooking. Choose a recipe you are familiar with or try a new one from a book, magazine or website.

Dream menu activity

Starter	**Drinks**
Main Course	**Drinks**
Dessert	**Drinks**

Menu planning activity

56 | Food II

Level A

Materials needed:

- All about food activity (see opposite)
- pen, paper (optional).

Discuss your food preferences, using the activity sheet to record your ideas.

Things to think about...

- Reasons you like, dislike or would like to try the foods you have chosen.
- How often do you eat your favourite foods?
- Do you think your tastes have changed over the years?

Level B

Materials needed:

- Different tastes activity (see opposite),
- pen, paper (optional).

Discuss the different foods on the activity sheet. Here are some questions to start with:

Things to think about...

- Have you ever tried these foods? If so, what did you think about them?
- Would you try any of these foods? Why? Why not?
- What do you think they would taste like?
- Can you group the foods into categories (i.e. seafood, meats)?
- Where might you find these foods?
- What kinds of food do you like or dislike?

All about food activity

Foods I like

Foods I dislike

Foods I would like to try

Different tastes activity

Jellied eels

Caviar

Frogs' legs

Blue cheese

Steak tartare (raw meat & egg)

Lamb's liver

Marmite

Oysters

Haggis

57 | Current Affairs I

Level A

Materials needed:

- Pen and paper (optional)
- container (optional).

Discuss topical issues in the news. You can write your chosen topics on slips of paper and put them in a container. Pull out questions at random to discuss.

Suggested topics…

- What do you think about mobile phones?
- Reports indicate that women are being assisted to have children much later in life. In your opinion, what is the ideal age to have children?
- Should rubbish collections be limited to once a fortnight?
- Obesity is a growing problem in the UK. Why do you think this is?

Level B

Materials needed:

- Recent newspapers, special supplements, local magazines, articles sourced from the internet.

Choose some articles about current news stories/current global or local issues to generate discussion.

Things to think about…

- Recent world events
- How events affect people in the area
- Can we learn anything from similar events from the past?

Current Affairs II | 58

Level A

Materials needed:

- Newspaper articles, radio news, TV news show, articles from the internet.

Discuss any areas of interest in the current news.

Things to think about...

- Have news items changed over the years?
- Has the way news is presented and reported changed at all?
- Where do you like to get your news from?
- Do you have a preferred newspaper? Are there any you dislike?

Level B

Materials needed:

- Local newsletters, letters received in the post (e.g. election candidate information, recycling information), information pamphlets, or articles sourced from the internet.

Discuss local news or upcoming events using local literature as a cue.

Things to think about...

- Any local news and how it might impact your community
- Local changes that are likely to take place
- Local policies such as recycling, parking, and neighbourhood watch

59 | Faces/Scenes I

Level A & Level B

Materials needed:

- Fashionable faces activity sheet (see below and opposite)
- pen and paper (optional).

Discuss the images of fashion styles on the activity sheets. This activity is focused on exploring opinions and associations. You might like to include some of your own photos in the activity, and compare these to the images provided, when discussing how your style has changed over the years.

Things to think about...

- Can you identify the fashion of each era? Would you try any of the outfits?
- What can you tell about a person just by looking at their face? (e.g. friendly, outgoing etc.)
- What sort of job do you think each person does?
- If you were to choose one as a friend, which one would it be and why?
- What are each face's best / worst features?
- Do you think the people in the images are representative of their era?
- Has your 'style' changed over the years?
- Who do you think is the most serious? carefree? casual? smart?

1940s
1970s

1980s

2000s

60 | Faces/Scenes II

Level A & Level B

Materials needed:

- Scenes activity (see below and opposite) or use your own pictures from magazines, calendars etc.

Examine and discuss the landscapes provided. You could add images from magazines or photos of your own.

Things to think about…

- Similarities and differences between the scenes
- Which one do you like best and why?
- Which one do you like the least and why?
- Have you ever visited any places like these?
- Would you want to visit any of these places?
- What sort of people might live, work in or visit these places?
- Which scenes look exotic?
- Which scenes look close to home?
- How would you expect to spend your time if you were visiting the place in the picture? Would you need to take anything in particular?

61 | Word Association I

Level A

Materials needed:

- Pen and paper (optional).

Choose a topic and think of words, ideas and things you associate with it (eg: Night time – sleeping, foxes and nocturnal animals, dark, stars, the moon etc.). The topic can be as broad or specialist as you like. You could create a mind map to show your ideas, or just have a discussion. See where your ideas take you.

Suggested topics…

- Holidays
- Paris
- The Prime Minister

Level B

Materials needed:

- Pen and paper (optional).

Have a game of free association. Begin with an agreed word and each take turns to say a word related to the last word said. For example, you might agree that 'dog' is your first word. The first player might say 'walk', the second player might say 'run', the first player takes another turn and might say 'race', the second player 'medal' and so on.

Before you begin, agree when the game will stop (e.g. after you have thought of 20 words, or run out of words).

Word Association II | 62

Level A

Materials needed:

- Famous pairs activity (see below)
- pen (optional).

Match each half of the well known pairs with their 'other halves'. Discuss the meaning of the pairs (e.g. what are 'bangers' and 'mash'?), any recollections you have of the pairs or any associations you can think of. Suggested answers can be found on page 157.

Level B

Pick a word or a concept and see how many other words you can think of with the same meaning. For example, the word 'happy', has a similar meaning to 'jolly', 'joyful', and 'cheerful'.

Alternatively...

You might like to revisit some of the activities from Sessions 35/36 or Session 61.

Famous pairs activity

Couples:

Romeo and....
Ginger and....
Cleopatra and....
Sonny and....
Queen Victoria and....
Bonnie and....
Robin Hood and....
Tarzan and....
Adam and....
Mickey Mouse and....
Beauty and....
Batman and....
Bill and....
Butch Cassidy and....
Richard and....
William and....

Companies:

Black and....
Johnson and....
Lea and....
Marks and...

Food:

Bangers and....
Salt and....
Fish and....
Strawberries and....
Tea and....
Bread and....
Apples and....
Bacon and....
Jelly and....
Cheese and....
Champagne and....
Rhubarb and....
Peaches and....
Bubble and....

Novels:

War and.....
Sense and....
Pride and....

63 | Being Creative I

Level A & Level B

Spend the session engaging in a creative activity together. You may want to consider some of the activities below depending on what materials you have available or what interests you and the person share…

- Baking, cake decorating or cooking
- Knitting, sewing, embroidering or cross-stitch
- Gardening (planting, watering, hanging baskets, herb gardens, window boxes, vegetable patches)
- Painting or drawing (paper, canvas, pot, plates etc.)
- Card making

…or you might have plenty of ideas of your own!

Being Creative I | 64

Level A & Level B

Continue with the Being Creative activity you started in session 7 or choose another from the list provided below.

Suggestions...

- Photo frame making, photography or photo collage
- Poems or short stories
- Flower arranging
- Model making (clay, plasticine)
- Music
- Patchwork quilt making
- Dancing
- Singing

65 | Categorising Objects I

Level A

Materials needed:
- Pen and paper (optional)
- timer (optional).

Think of categories and list as many examples as you can in each category. For example, if you chose flowers as a category, you might list roses, lilies, violets, daisies etc.

Suggestions...
- Things you might take on a picnic
- Things you would find at the seaside
- Types of bird
- Types of cheese or fruit
- Countries
- Things to do on a sunny day

Level B

Materials needed:
- Timer (optional).

Think of categories and list as many examples as you can by setting a timer and see how many words you can think of within the time set. You can choose more specific categories:

- Things to do on a sunny day in the town centre
- Fruit with stones
- Birds native to the British Isles

Categorising Objects I | 66

Level A

Materials needed:

- Objects from around the house, or images of objects from magazines /catalogues
- pen and paper (optional).

Collect some objects together from around the home or pictures of objects and group the items together in different ways. For example, the odd one out, all objects of the same colour, objects from the same room etc.

Level B

Materials needed:

- Pen and paper (optional)
- timer (optional).

Think of words beginning with a certain letter in a category, for example:

- Girls' names beginning with 'S'
- Animals beginning with 'P'

You may want to write your ideas down. You could set a timer to make the game more challenging.

67 | Orientation I

Level A

Materials needed:

- Landscapes activity (see pages 135-6)
- images of landscapes from books/magazines (optional).

Discuss the landscapes using the following topics as a guide:

Things to think about…

- Would you like to visit any of these landscapes? Why?
- Are there any you wouldn't like to visit? Why?
- Is there anything special about these landscapes?
- Would you like to live in any of these places?

Level B

Materials needed:

- Landscapes activity (see pages 135-6),
- world map
- images/photos from holidays or magazines.

Discuss the landscapes using the topics below as a guide:

Things to think about…

- Where might you expect to find these landscapes?
- Are these landscapes similar or different to each other?
- What do you think you would need to live in these conditions? (e.g. warm clothes)
- Do you think any of the landscapes are popular tourist sites? Why, or why not?

Alternatively…

Create a list of landmarks you have visited. Look at and discuss photos you have from these places.

Orientation I | 67

67 | Orientation I

Orientation II | 68

Level A

Materials needed:
- Around the UK activity sheet (see pages 138-139)
- UK map (optional)
- pen (optional).

Discuss where in the UK you might find the foods, objects and places shown on the activity sheets.

Things to think about...
- Where might you find these places or objects?
- What would you associate these things with? For example you might associate fish and chips with the seaside or a Friday tea time treat.
- Do the images bring back any memories?

Level B

Materials needed:
- Town map game (see pages 140-141)
- scissors (optional)
- dice, counters (or coins).

Play the town map board game together as a team, or against each other. Pick a destination on the town map. The objective of the game is to get from Bus Stop F (bottom left hand corner of the board) to your chosen destination (i.e. the cinema, the bank). Throw a dice and move a coin or counter to the number of places shown. You can move around the board in any direction, including backwards.

If you land on a coloured or patterned square, turn to the 'key cards' on page 141, which give instructions or tasks for the player. If you land on a purple 'bus ride' square you may move to the 'bus stop' square of your choice.

68 | Orientation II

Around the UK

Orientation II | 68

68 | Orientation II

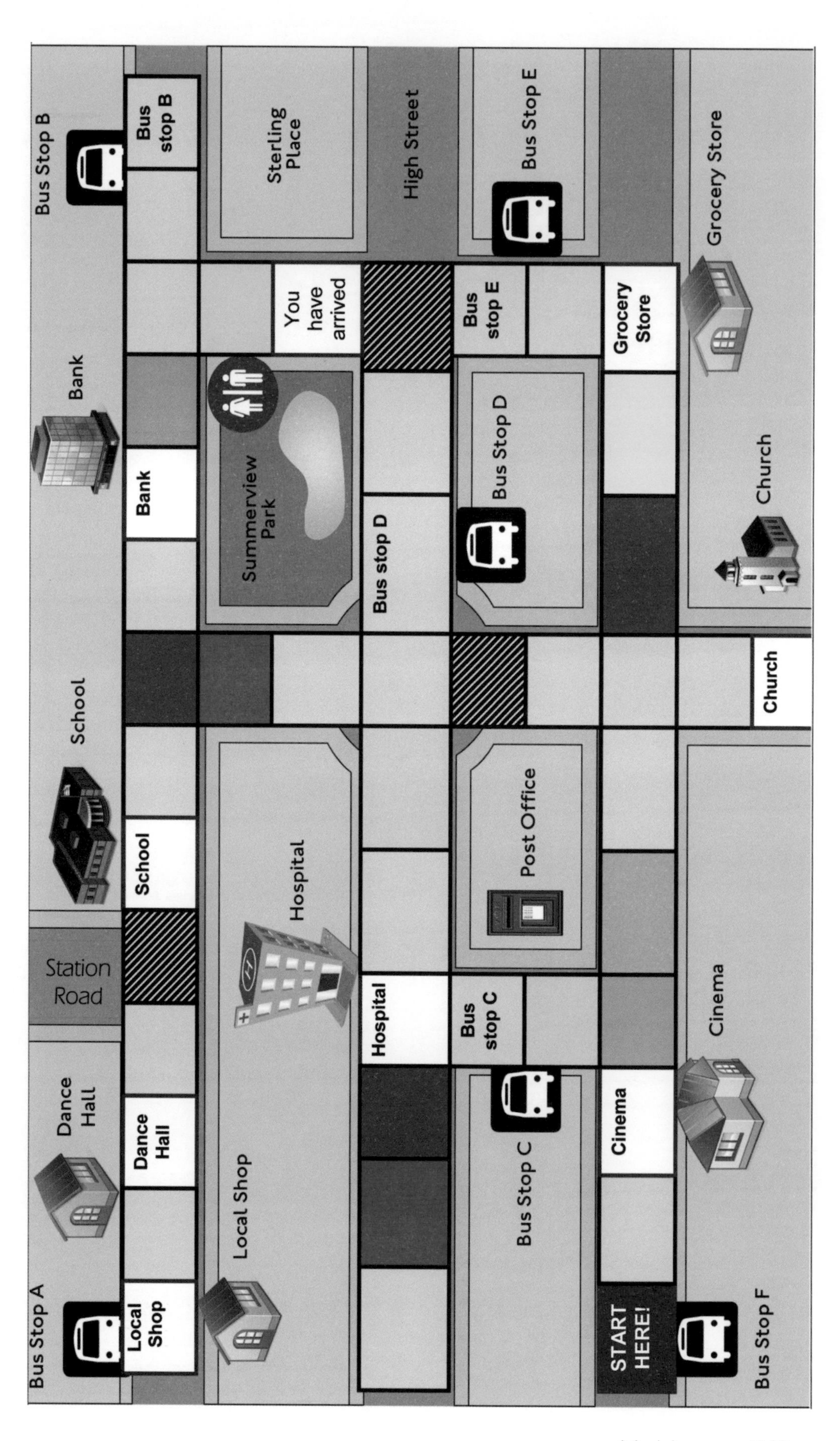

Town Map Game Key Cards

ROADWORKS There are roadworks in your way! Move back 2 spaces to avoid them.	**GREEN LIGHT** The traffic lights are green, move ahead 1 space.
RED LIGHT The traffic lights are red, miss a go.	**BUS RIDE** Move to any of the bus stops on the board.
POST OFFICE Can you name 3 things associated with the post office?	**PARK** Can you name 3 things you might see in a park?
GROCERY STORE Name 3 things you might buy if you went into the grocery store.	**CINEMA** What kind of films do you like to watch?

69 | Using Money I

Level A & Level B

Materials needed:

- Container, pen and paper (optional).

Discuss the following questions related to money:

- You find a £5 note on the street – what do you do?
- What would you do if you won the lottery?
- Do you think purchasing items on credit is a good idea?
- Do you agree with the saying 'Health is better than wealth' or 'Money is the root of all evil'?
- Are you a 'saver' or a 'spender'?
- What is your opinion on betting and gambling? Would you ever lend money to anyone?
- Do you agree with the saying 'Look after the pennies and the pounds will look after themselves'?

You can think of questions of your own, or pick a selection of the above questions. Write the questions on paper, fold them up and put them in a container so that you can pick them out at random. Share ideas and opinions and any anecdotes or personal experiences you have related to the questions.

Using Money II | 70

Level A

Materials needed:
- Pen and paper (optional).

Discuss the following questions related to money, or add any of your own.

Suggestions...
- Should children be given pocket money? Were you given pocket money?
- Do you think we should have a minimum wage? What should it be?
- Do you think some professions deserve to earn more?
- Do you have a favourite charity? If so, why did you choose to support it?
- What kinds of things should the government spend money on? (e.g. NHS, schools)
- What kinds of things do you like to spend your money on?

Level B

Materials needed:
- Pen and paper (optional).

Plan a visit or a trip to a place of interest:

- What would you need to buy before/during the visit?
- How much would your purchases cost? (e.g. bus fare)
- How would you pay? Would you draw out money from the bank or pay with a card?

You could either begin with a set budget or add up the total cost of your trip at the end.

71 | Number Games I

Level A

Materials needed:
• Pen and paper (optional).

Counting game: Take a look around the room you are in, and count how many of the following items you can see...

Suggestions...
• Objects that are blue
• Circular objects
• Photographs
• Electrical appliances
• Objects used for leisure

Level B

Materials needed:
• Playing cards and dominoes
• number based board games
• pen and paper.

Below are some suggestions:

• card games e.g. Snap!, Pontoon
• higher or lower (guess whether the next card in the deck will have a higher or lower value)
• bingo
• dominoes

Number Games II | 72

Level A & Level B

Materials needed:
- Playing cards and dominoes
- number based board games
- pen and paper
- container and contents to count (optional).

Revisit some of the number games you particularly enjoyed from previous sessions. Below are some suggestions:

- Ludo
- Connect 4
- Yahtzee
- Noughts and crosses
- Guess how many items in a container e.g. chocolates in a box, pennies in a jar, count them and see whose guess is the closest!

73 | Word Games I

Level A & Level B

Materials needed:

- Word games from magazines, puzzle books or newspapers (optional)
- pen, paper
- word based board games (optional).

Revisit some of the word games you particularly enjoyed from previous sessions. Below are some suggestions:

- Hangman: Think of a word, film, song title or famous person and draw a number of dashes for each letter of the word/name. Guess the missing letters. Incorrect letters contribute to the drawing of a 'hangman' and losing the game.
- Complete a word game from a newspaper together e.g. crossword, word search.
- Taboo: think of a word for your partner to guess, and try to describe it without using the word itself. E.g. if the word were 'dog', you might say 'an animal', 'four legs', 'barks'. You could both write ideas for words on slips of folded paper and put them in a hat.

Word Games II | 74

Level A & Level B

Materials needed:

- Word games from magazines, puzzle books or newspapers (optional)
- pen, paper
- word based board games (optional).

Revisit some of the word games you particularly enjoyed from previous sessions. Below are some suggestions:

- Words-within-a-word game: think of a long word with lots of different letters in (e.g. submarine, paleontological, onomatopoeia, continental) and see how many smaller words you can make from it.
- Prefixes game: think of as many words as you can beginning with a common prefix such as PRE-, CON-, PRO-, IN-etc.
- Recite the alphabet out loud attaching a word to each letter (e.g. A- ant, B- boy, C- car). If you want to make the game more challenging, try to think of more than one word for each letter.
- Scrabble
- Other board-based word games you may have.

75 | Quiz

Level A & Level B

Materials needed:

- Quiz board game (see opposite)
- coin or counter
- dice.

Take turns to roll the dice and move on the quiz board game. Answer the questions or follow the instructions given in the box you land on. The first person to reach the finish at the top of the board wins the game!

Alternatively....
Play a game you both enjoy.

Suggestions...

- Guess what I'm miming, often known as Charades
- Guess what I'm drawing, often known as Pictionary
- Board games
- Quizzes.

36. **FINISH!**	35.	34. **Name 4 pieces of clothing**	33. *Move ahead to the finish line to win the game!*	32.	31. Describe the person you are with
25 *Move ahead to box number 27*	26. Describe yourself	27.	28. **Name 4 occupations**	29.	30.
24.	23.	22. **Name 4 hobbies**	21. Describe the room you are in	20. **Name 3 famous people**	19.
13. Describe the weather today	14. **Name 4 types of tree**	15.	16.	17. * Move ahead 3 spaces	18. **Name 4 colours**
12. **Name 3 wild animals**	11.	10. *Move ahead to Box number 14*	9.	8. **Name 3 countries**	7. *Move ahead 2 spaces*
1. **START HERE**	2.	3.	4.	5. Describe how you feel today	6.

Answers

11 Quiz Games 1

Old Wives' Tales Quiz:

Eating before you swim causes cramp: FALSE
Eating just before swimming does not increase risk of cramp. However, it is recommended that you should wait for digestion to begin if you have eaten a particularly fatty meal.

Sitting too close to the television will ruin your eyes: FALSE
Sitting too close to the TV will not cause any deterioration of the eyes.

Carrots are good for your eyesight: TRUE
Carrots contain beta-carotene and Vitamin A, which can help prevent degeneration of the eyes.

You will catch a cold if you go out on a chilly night with wet hair: FALSE
The only way to catch a cold virus is by coming into direct contact with the virus itself.

Sugar makes children hyperactive: FALSE
Research suggests this is not the case! It may be that the environment the child is in is the defining factor in how lively their mood is.

An apple a day keeps the doctor away: TRUE
Healthy foods like fruit and vegetables boost the immune system and could help protect against cancer.

Lightning never strikes in the same place twice: FALSE
Lightning can strike the same place numerous times. The Empire State Building is hit an average of 25 times a year!

Gain a child, lose a tooth: TRUE
Researchers from New York University College of Dentistry found that pregnancy can increase the risk of developing gum disease, which can lead to tooth loss.

General Knowledge Quiz:

c) Flower
b) Elephant
b) Statue of Liberty
a) Red
a) Coronation Street
a) Cleanliness
c) Nine
b) Prince Phillip
c) Rowing
b) Giant wave
c) Raven
b) Stamp

Answers

12 Quiz Games II

Music Quiz

Matching lyrics to the artist and filling in the blanks:

Don't sit under the apple tree – Glenn Miller Band
Apple, anyone, sit, apple, marchin'

On the street where you live – Nat King Cole
Street, pavement, storeys, street, live

We'll Meet Again – Vera Lynn
Where, when, sunny, smiling, skies

Pennies from Heaven – Bing Crosby
Rains, pennies, cloud, pennies

I've got you under my skin – Frank Sinatra
Skin, deep, part, under, skin

Return to Sender – Elvis Presley
Sender, number, coming back

Pretty Woman – Roy Orbison
Woman, woman, like, woman, truth, good

Magic Moments – Perry Como
Moments, moments, memories, forget, night, ride

Que sera sera – Doris Day
Little, mother, pretty, sera, sera, future's, will be

You're nobody till somebody loves you – Dean Martin
Nobody, loves, cares, gold, happiness

13 Sounds I

Sounds effects activity

By track number:
1. Snoring
2. Birdsong
3. Breaking glass
4. Baby cooing
5. Cat meowing
6. Church bell
7. Cuckoo clock
8. Ducks
9. Fly buzzing
10. Horse neighing
11. Squeaky kiss
12. Laughter
13. Telephone ringing
14. Pinball machine
15. Cash register
16. Train whistling

Answers

14 Sounds II

Styles of Music activity

By track number:
1. Blues
2. Classical
3. World
4. Funk
5. Jazz
6. Reggae
7. Rock
8. Salsa
9. Country
10. Waltz

18 Categorising Objects II

Odd one out series

Visual series 1: Fox is the odd one out as the rest are members of the cat family

Visual series 2: Coins are the odd one out as they do not float.

Visual series 3: Piano is the odd one out as the rest are string instruments.

Visual series 4: The landscape on the bottom right hand side of the page is the odd one out as it does not show any water.

Number series 1: 11 is the odd one out as it does not contain the number '5'

Concept series 1: Monsoon is the odd one out as it is just rain, the rest are windy conditions

Concept series 2: Love is the odd one out as it is a positive emotion, the rest are negative emotions

Concept series 3: Crocus is the odd one out as it begins with the letter 'C'

21 Useful Tips I

Useful Household Tips activity

To stop a door from squeaking…
… use a non-stick cooking spray to grease the hinges

To remove a dirty ring around a shirt collar…
… apply shampoo to the area.

To make threading a needle easier…
… apply hairspray to the thread, when it is dry it will stiffen enough to pass easily through the eye.

To cure a headache…
… cut a lime in half and rub it on your forehead.

To prevent new patent leather shoes from cracking…
… rub with vaseline.

To kill and repel bedbugs…
…. apply bacon dripping to the area.

To prevent potatoes from sprouting…
… place an apple in the bag with them.

To soothe a sore throat…
… take some honey.

31 Word Games I

Proverbs word game

… deep
… choosers
… never
… sorry
… is a friend indeed
… comes a calm
… after supper walk a mile
… a good ending
… at home
… itself
… where the heart is
… the best policy
… than vinegar
… his tools
… shy
… don't
… day
… due
… neighbours
… fools seldom differ

32 Word Games II

Word Search Activity

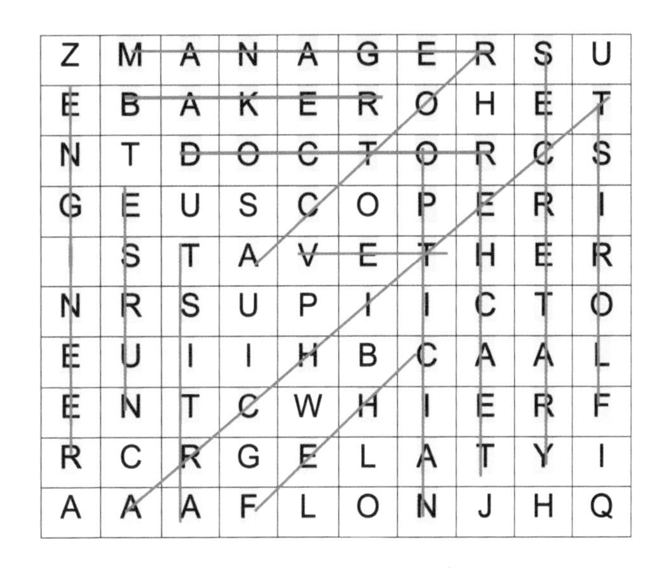

Z	M	A	N	A	G	E	R	S	U
E	B	A	K	E	R	O	H	E	T
N	T	D	O	C	T	O	R	C	S
G	E	U	S	C	O	P	E	R	I
	S	T	A	V	E	T	H	E	R
N	R	S	U	P	I	I	C	T	O
E	U	I	I	H	B	C	A	A	L
E	N	T	C	W	H	I	E	R	F
R	C	R	G	E	L	A	T	Y	I
A	A	A	F	L	O	N	J	H	Q

33 Slogans I

Slogan matching activity

In the order the slogans appear on the activity sheet:
Zanussi
Abbey National
Clairol Hair Colouring
Coca-Cola
Courage Beer
ESSO Gasoline
Smash Instant Potato
Kelloggs Frosties
Gillette
Hoover Vacuum Cleaners
Fairy Liquid
Kentucky Fried Chicken
L'Oreal
Mars
Remington

Answers

Yellow Pages
Cadbury's Flake
Rice Krispies

34 Slogans II

Matching logos with brands activity

From the top to the bottom of the pages:
Fairy Liquid
Green Giant
Shell
Mercedes
World Wildlife Fund
McDonald's
Penguin books
Marks & Spencer
Oxfam
Rolls Royce

35 Associated Words I

Associated pairs activity

Amounts
Cup of... **tea / coffee**
Loaf of... **bread**
Slice of... **bread, cake, ham, life etc.**
Jug of... **water, milk, beer etc.**
Pint of... **milk, beer etc.**
Gallon of... **petrol**
Reel of... **cotton**
Ball of... **wool**
Pair of... **shoes, trousers, glasses**
Bucket of... **water, sand**

Couples
Laurel and... **Hardy**
Morecambe and... **Wise**
Little and... **Large**

Places
Westminster... **Abbey**
Buckingham... **Palace**
Windsor... **Castle**
Trafalgar... **Square**
Piccadilly... **Circus**
Nelson's... **Column**
Waterloo... **Station**
Canterbury... **Cathedral**
Charing... **Cross**
New... **York, Orleans, -castle**
Times... **Square**
Capitol... **Hill**

General
Flora and... **Fauna**
Bed and... **Breakfast**
Bow and... **Arrow**
Breaking and... **Entering**
Cats and... **Dogs**
Chalk and... **Cheese**
Day and... **Night**
Heaven and... **Hell / Earth**
Left and... **Right**

36 Associated Words II

Proverbs activity

... saves nine
... the sun shines
... boils
... on the other side
... two in the bush
... hot
... make light work
... spoil the broth
... in one basket
... grow fonder
... out of mind
... spilt milk
... to spite your face
... in the fire
... in the mouth
... you might just get it
... of the beholder
... grow
... lie
... wins
... try and try again
... bliss
... medicine

Proverbs crossword

ACROSS:
1. The more you get the more you WANT
4. Strike while the iron is HOT
5. Old habits DIE hard
7. Many hands MAKE light work
10. There's no fool like an OLD fool
12. Love conquers ALL
13. Do as I SAY, not as I do

DOWN:
2. All's fair in love AND war
3. You can't win THEM all
6. Barking DOGS seldom bite
8. ALL in a day's work
9. Money is the root of all EVIL
11. Every dog has his DAY

40 Using Money II

Foreign Currency activity

UK – Pound Sterling
Europe – Euro
Japan – Yen
India – Rupee
Russia – Ruble
America – Dollar

Answers

43 Art Discussion 1

Self portraits activity

Vincent Van Gogh

Frida Kahlo

Andy Warhol

Tamara de Lempicka

Pablo Picasso

Henri Matisse

Salvador Dali

45 My Life (Occupations) 1

Professions activity

Painter / Decorator
Pilot
Doctor
Gardener
Fireman
Chef
Carpenter
Teacher

51 Sounds 1

Musical instruments activity

1) Bass
2) Drums
3) Flute
4) Guitar
5) Organ
6) Piano
7) Triangle
8) Trumpet
9) Xylophone
10) Tambourine

Answers

53 Childhood I

Childhood toys activity

First column, top to bottom:
Pick up sticks
Cup and ball
Hoopla

Second column, top to bottom:
Yo-yo
Jacks
Diabolo
Skipping Rope

Third column, top to bottom:
Conkers
Spinning tops
Tic-tac-toe

62 Word Association II

Famous pairs activity

Couples:
Romeo and... **Juliet**
Ginger and... **Fred**
Cleopatra and... **Antony**
Sonny and... **Cher**
Queen Victoria and... **Prince Albert**
Bonnie and... **Clyde**
Robin Hood and... **Maid Marion**
Tarzan and... **Jane**
Adam and... **Eve**
Mickey Mouse and... **Minnie Mouse**
Beauty and... **The Beast**
Batman and... **Robin**
Bill and... **Ben**
Butch Cassidy and... **The Sundance Kid**
Richard and... **Judy**
William and... **Mary / Kate**

Companies:
Black and... **Decker**
Johnson and... **Johnson**
Lea and... **Perrins**
Marks and... **Spencer**

(continued on page 158)

Answers

Food:
Bangers and... **mash**
Salt and... **pepper / vinegar**.
Fish and... **chips**
Strawberries and... **cream**
Tea and... **biscuits / cake / coffee**
Bread and... **butter / water**
Apples and... **pears**
Bacon and... **eggs**
Jelly and... **custard**
Cheese and... **biscuits / wine**
Champagne and... **strawberries**
Rhubarb and... **custard**
Peaches and... **cream**
Bubble and... **squeak**

Novels:
War and... **Peace**
Sense and... **Sensibility**
Pride and... **Prejudice**

About the authors

Lauren Yates is a research assistant at North East London Foundation Trust (NELFT), and PhD student at University College London (UCL). Part of Professor Orrell's team since 2009, she was involved in the Maintenance CST trial, prior to working on iCST. Having family affected by dementia, she decided the best way to put her experience to good use was to pursue a career in dementia care research, with the hope of helping families like hers to seek support, and to provide a better standard of care for carers and people with dementia.

Professor Martin Orrell is Professor of Ageing and Mental Health at University College London (UCL) and a Consultant Old Age Psychiatrist at North East London Foundation Trust. He leads several major research programmes to develop and evaluate psychosocial interventions for dementia care. He has published over 200 academic papers and is Editor of the journal Aging & Mental Health.

Phuong Leung completed her MSc degree in Aging and Mental Health from University College London (UCL) in 2010, and joined the iCST multicentre randomised trial for people with dementia in 2011 as a research assistant. She was actively involved in developing and designing the activity workbook. Prior to getting involved in dementia research, she was working with vulnerable older people and people with dementia in the community for 12 years as an outreach and mental health promotion worker. Phuong is interested in adapting CST to other cultures. She recently provided CST cultural adaptations training to health care professionals in Hong Kong. She is also conducting a PhD investigating the effects of iCST and other dementia cognition-focused interventions for family carers of people with dementia."

Dr Aimee Spector was the lead researcher in the original developed CST trial. Since then she has published extensive research papers in relation to old age psychology, the CST training manual and leads the CST training course. She is now a Senior Lecturer in Clinical Psychology at University College London (UCL).

Bob Woods is Professor of Clinical Psychology of Older People at Bangor University and Director of the Dementia Services Development Centre Wales. He has published numerous books and academic papers in relation to old age psychology and dementia care and is an Alzheimer's Society Ambassador.

Dr Vasiliki Orgeta is a research psychologist interested in emotional well-being in late life, particularly in people with dementia and their carers. Her research focuses on systematic reviews of psychosocial interventions in dementia and MCI, and the development and evaluation of these interventions using RCTs. She led the development of iCST and the multi-centre randomised trial evaluating this approach, funded by Health and Technology Assessment. She works as a Senior Research Associate in the Division of Psychiatry, at University College London.

Acknowledgements

The Individual Cognitive Stimulation Therapy (iCST) Programme (ISRCTN 65945963) was funded by the NIHR Programme Grants for Applied Research funding scheme. The grantholders are Professors Orrell (UCL), Woods (Bangor), Burns (Manchester), Moniz-Cook (Hull), Russell (Swansea), Knapp (LSE), Dr. Aimee Spector (UCL), and Ms. Gillian Lasocki.

This manual presents independent research commissioned by the National Institute for Health Research Health Technology Assessment (NIHR HTA) programme (project number 08/116/06). The views expressed in this publication are those of the authors and not necessarily those of UCL, the NHS, the NIHR or the Department of Health.

The authors would like to thank the people with dementia, family caregivers, staff and professionals who took part in the iCST research study for their time and contribution.

The authors would also like to thank all of their colleagues at North East London Foundation Trust (NELFT) and UCL for their support and enthusiasm.

The iCST DVD

The iCST team would like to thank the following people who contributed to the production of the iCST DVD:

- The carers and people with dementia featuring in the footage who generously offered their time and did such an excellent job of demonstrating iCST sessions and techniques.
- Matt Caswell and Yahyia Mahmoud (Piers Video) who filmed and edited the sessions, and provided invaluable guidance both on set, and in the editing suite.
- Professor Martin Orrell, Dr. Aimee Spector, and Amy Streater who, as experts in the field of Cognitive Stimulation Therapy, were consulted about the edits of the footage.